The Growth and
Development of Mothers

The Growth

and Development of Mothers

ANGELA BARRON McBRIDE

PERENNIAL LIBRARY

HARPER & ROW, PUBLISHERS

New York, Evanston, San Francisco, London

This book was originally published by Harper & Row, Publishers, Inc. in 1973.

Grateful acknowledgment is made to the publishers for permission to reprint excerpts from the following:

The Art of Loving, copyright © 1956 by Erich Fromm. Published by Harper & Row.

Childhood and Adolescence: A Psychology of the Growing Person by L. Joseph Stone and Joseph Church, copyright © 1957 by Random House. Published by Random House.

The Collected Works of Henrik Ibsen, Volume VII, translated by William Archer. Published by Charles Scribner's Sons.

Man's World, Woman's Place, copyright © 1971 by Elizabeth Janeway. Published by William Morrow & Co.

The Marriage Relationship: Psychoanalytic Perspectives, edited by Salo Rosenbaum and Ian Alger, copyright © 1968 by the Society of Medical Psychoanalysts. Excerpted from Chapter 9 by Theodore Lidz. Published by Basic Books.

The Pursuit of Loneliness, copyright © 1970 by Philip Slater. Published by Beacon Press.

The Second Sex by Simone de Beauvoir, copyright © 1952 by Alfred A. Knopf, Inc. Published by Alfred A. Knopf.

Up the Sandbox, copyright © 1970 by Ann Richardson Roiphe. Published by Simon and Schuster.

The selections from *Mister Rogers* lyrics are used by permission of Fred Rogers and Small World Enterprises, Inc., and are excerpted from the following songs: "I'm Taking Care of You," copyright © 1968 by Fred Rogers; "Everything Grows Together" by Fred Rogers, copyright © 1968 by Small World Enterprises, Inc.; "When the Baby Comes," by Fred Rogers, copyright © 1967 by Small World Enterprises, Inc.; and "It's You I Like," copyright © 1971 by Fred Rogers.

Designed by Patricia Dunbar

First PERENNIAL LIBRARY edition published 1974.

STANDARD BOOK NUMBER: 06-080328-2

For my husband, Bill.
By asking me "What do you
want to do next?" he made
me aware of my future.

Contents

Acknowledgments

The research resources of the Yale University School of Nursing facilitated my survey of the literature on motherhood. Virginia Nehring and Donna Diers were especially helpful in bringing pertinent articles and books to my attention.

I am indebted to my colleagues, Rhetaugh Dumas and Virginia Henderson, to my sister, Cecilia Barron, to my parents, John and Mary Barron, to my secretary, Dolores Leona, and to my good friend Aileen Findlay, for their support and encouragement throughout this project. My thanks to Kitty Benedict for her helpful editorial suggestions.

The expertise of my husband, William McBride, in social philosophy influenced my thinking tremendously; he encouraged me every step of the way to formulate the questions that are explored in this book.

My daughters deserve a special loving thank you for teaching me so much. In very concrete ways, their well-timed hugs, their "happy face" drawings, and their "cheer up, Mommy" dances sustained me throughout this writing period.

Introduction

The other day, I asked my older daughter what she wanted to be when she grew up. Like generations of little girls before her, she said, "I want to get married, be a good mommy, and have babies of my own to play with." Inside myself, I laughed and cried as she answered. What made me ask the ritual question, and what caused her to give the ritual response? What does it mean to be a "good" mommy? What would Women's Lib think of me and my daughter? Why didn't my daughter say she wanted to be a dentist, a dancer, or a photographer instead? Was her answer prompted by a desire to imitate me or by some vague notion that little girls are not supposed to have careers? Are we in fact ever "grown up" enough to have babies? In that one moment, all my thoughts and feelings about being a mother paraded in front of me. I ached to tell her that you are never "grown up" and that I was somehow lying to her in even asking the question. Being a "good" mommy is an impossible job. Well, in true five-year-old fashion, Cammie interrupted my reverie to ask if she could go outside and play. But I kept on pondering what she had said.

The "live happily ever after" quality of Cammie's words touched me. Even in college my ideas about being a wife, a mother, and having children were not very different from those of my daughter. Being a wife and a mother were prizes to be won. Love and reverence would automatically descend. I could smile deferentially on my husbandless, childless friends and complain about all the ironing and cooking that I had to do, but everyone would know that I would never exchange my rose-covered, polished world for theirs. In fact, being able to bitch in a pious way about all the work was part of the prize.

I went into nursing because it would be a "good" preparation for wifehood and motherhood. Where is the man who does not find a caring woman in white beautiful? My relatives regularly mentioned that a nursing background would always be useful, even if you get married right after school. All mothers have to deal with scratches and bruises and upset stomachs. "You can use your psychology on your kids," some said. So I became a nurse, not because it is an interesting profession in its own right (which it certainly is), but because "it's something to fall back on in case you marry a drunkard," and "such a feminine profession." The assumption made by most of my friends and relatives was that you would never want to work after you had children unless your husband died or you married an alcoholic. After all, motherhood is the *ultimate fulfillment.* I grew up with an honor-roll mentality, and I never lost sight of the fact that a man to support me for life and father my children would be my crowning achievement.

But tragedy struck. I was not engaged by my twenty-first birthday. With college and an R.N. behind me, I decided that my only hope of getting married was to transplant myself into a predominantly male environment. I went to Yale University to do graduate work in psychiatric nursing, and this time I was successful. I landed a husband, and here I am seven years later with two daughters: Cammie, five, and Kara, two.

Here I am. My mother and father are proud of me because I married a nonalcoholic Ph.D. of the same religion. The *Ladies' Home Journal* would be proud of me for going to Europe for the first time on my honeymoon and having the man of my dreams point out to me the pleasures of France and Italy. Zero Population Growth is proud of me because I have only two children. The natural-childbirth people should be proud of me because I used the various breathing exercises during labor and delivery, and nursed both babies. My pediatrician is proud of me because both children have gotten the various immunizations at the approved time. My friends are proud of me because we bought a house with an unusually low mortgage interest rate, and I have even learned how to stain unpainted furniture so we could decorate our home quite economically. I can cook fancy meals, keep track of relatives' birthdays, and give children's parties without the guests crying.

But am I living happily ever after? Yes and no. I have a loving, understanding husband, two pretty and bright children, and I regularly feel like screaming, "Why didn't anyone ever tell me that no one lives happily ever after?" Why do fairy tales always end with the prince and princess marrying? Why don't they tell you what happened to the couple in the next fifty years? How did the prince and princess feel when the babies started coming? Did Cinderella ever wake up in the morning to the cry of her baby, feeling as evil and fussy as her stepsisters? How much growing up did the prince and princess have to do to help their children grow up?

Growing up . . . that's what being a child is all about and that's what being a parent is all about. In the process of trying to understand myself in these new relationships, I have become more and more convinced that we have to talk about the growth and development of parents whenever we talk about the growth and development of children, because the two are so interrelated. I guess that is why I wanted to tell my daughter that we are never really "grown up." We all tend to think about getting married and having babies in a vague, dreamy way, but getting used to living with another adult in a loving give-and-take atmosphere takes a good deal of effort. You have to rethink who you are in relation to the other person. Living with children in a loving give-and-take fashion requires even more work and effort, because it is the first time most of us have ever been called upon to be truly unselfish.

Too many writers either assume that maturity is automatically bestowed upon a human being by virtue of producing offspring, or they are busy describing what qualities the parent should develop for the sake of the child. Traditionally, mother has been given little opportunity to say that she is someone "in process" herself. (I use the feminine gender because the mother is usually seen as the primary parent in our society, and my own emphasis will be on the mother. Yet what I say about the mother is equally true of the father.) Parents incorporate stereotyped thinking into their own behavior and feel inadequate because they fall so short of those mythical creatures—the good mother, the unselfish provider, the understanding wife, the patient husband. Even those who talk about "ego integrity" or "maturity" as the goal of the adult years describe the developmental issues of this period in a very sketchy way. They are curiously silent about what it really looks and feels like to be "grown up." Little anecdotal material is available on the growth and development of the parent while she encourages the growth and development of her child. In fact, many authors seem to imply that survival is about all you can expect during your child's preschool years.

I am convinced that parenthood is a role you *grow into* by understanding your own behavior and by learning how to handle your own needs. To understand yourself you have to figure out what part of you still clings to fairy tales, to one-dimensional notions of life. You have to try to come to terms with your own faults and strengths while you help your children deal with their problems and possibilities. You have to realize in your gut that you will never be a storybook parent because storybooks don't allow for flux and change. Besides, you don't have storybook children!

I want to write first about some of my own thoughts and feelings about growing as a parent, that I could not describe to Cammie. There are some crucial issues I think a mother has to be aware of if she wants to facilitate the child's development. Specifics may vary from person to person, but certain themes are common to the experience of all parents. For the mother to mature, I believe she has to come to terms with society's expectations of her and the expectations she has for herself, her husband, and children. For example, you have to be clear about all those "normal crazy" reasons why you had a baby before you can deal with the child's reality in the fullest possible way. The woman who expects a child to provide her with the "ultimate fulfillment" (and all mothers have internalized this hope to some extent) is bound to feel frustrated and cheated. Since our society foolishly holds the mother responsible for "keeping the family happy" (as one text puts it), every mother must sort out the possible from the impossible so that she does not feel completely overwhelmed by a million and one "oughts."

In the middle chapters, I consider some of the emotions all parents have to struggle with. Anger, depression, guilt, and ambivalence are feelings that plague all mothers, but we are inclined to ignore their existence because "grown-ups" are not supposed to indulge such emotions. Yet how successful we are in living with these feelings determines the kind of support we can offer our children. So many of the feelings that a parent has are tied up with the fact that the child is a kind of extension of the parent. Much of what we feel about ourselves is projected onto our children. Looking at the reflection of your "self" in the child can be either frightening or flattering, but, most of all—and what we usually do not realize—it can be a big help in assessing your own developmental needs. But instead of thinking through why we expect impossible perfection in ourselves and our children, we mothers alternate between going around in emotional circles and struggling for rigid control over the reactions and behavior of our children. Rather than denying what bothers us, emphasis should be placed on documenting the "normal crazy" thoughts, impulses, and fantasies that the child's experiences provoke in the parent so they can be better understood.

In Chapter 6, I use the Oedipal-Electra period of the child's development to illustrate the developmental needs of the parent during a specific phase of the child's life. The interest of the child in sexual matters, the child's attraction to the parent of the opposite sex and eventual indentification with the parent of the same sex stir up all sorts of memories and passions in the parent, which—if handled on a conscious level—can lead to reciprocal growth and maturity. My hunch is that if you are aware of what you and your child are going through together, you are in a better position to try out new ways of behaving and to act reasonably.

But trying out new ways of behaving is, in turn, tied up with whether or not the society we live in permits variety and experimentation. The more I thought about my five-year-old's words, and the more I thought about what it means to be "grown up" and a "good mommy," the more I became impressed with how much our personal confusion about roles, our muddled emotions, and our overwhelming desire to develop the miracle child are related to the thinking of the community-at-large. Any coming to terms with your "self" must include some questioning of the pressures and expectations society imposes on you. If the parent is to realize her human potential, she has to live in a society that permits all its members to maximize their human potential (her child's included). A society is only as open and stimulating as individuals allow it to be. So the truly "grown-up" mother has to help society "grow up" too. And, in saying this, I have just come full circle from my daughter's original remark. Her words set me to thinking about my own frustrations and how much I have to "grow up" so she can develop. I have thought a good deal and felt even more, and I know that it is easier to holler about the frustrations of being a mother than to change the role, but change it we must, if living *somewhat* happily ever after is going to be a possibility for any of our children. Fashionable (but *very* important) talk about Women's Lib, or promoting mental health, or consciousness-raising should encourage all of us to use our real experiences as mothers to move away from a world where individuals find it easier to adopt a cardboard, ready-made image than to create one. The mature person defines herself; she is not defined by others.

This book moves from personal awareness to social awareness and back again. The various mood changes in the book reflect, I think, the seesaw quality of most mothers' experiences. My blending of anecdotal material with criticism of the child-rearing and psychoanalytic literature also points out, I hope, that any treatment of the mother has to speak to both the experiential and the intellectual elements in her role.

Finally, let me emphasize that this is not a how-to-do-it book. I do not pretend to be an expert on raising children (neither are most parents or professionals). At most, I know something about little girls up to the age of five. My reflections are meant to be provocative and suggestive. I have tried to put my thoughts and feelings into a framework of growth and development that makes some sense out of my own experiences, and I hope that my conclusions and criticisms will spur other parents to think about what they are going through as their children mature. I do not look forward to an era of test-tube babies so women can cease to be burdened by motherhood, but I do look forward to the day when parents of both sexes can talk about their experiences without idealizing them or emphasizing only those emotions and impulses that reinforce some impossible notion of parents and children living "happily ever after." Maybe we can start talking about people having all sorts of good, bad, fussy, and joyous moments in their lives. Perhaps the day is fast approaching when children's stories will begin with the prince and princess getting married, and not end there? That would show that both society and parents were really "grown up."

That the child is the supreme aim of woman is a statement having precisely the value of an advertising slogan. . . . There is an extravagant fraudulence in the easy reconciliation made between the common attitude of contempt for women and the respect shown for mothers.

—*Simone de Beauvoir*[1]*

1
The Motherhood Mystique

Thanks to Betty Friedan, American women woke up to the fact that a "feminine mystique" existed, which limited the role satisfaction, educational opportunities, and life possibilities of all women. Her exposition of the impact of functionalism and Freudian theory on modern woman's identity problem is excellent, but she failed to take into account the extent of the "motherhood mystique" in this country and its effect on women. As many other writers have done, she refers to the social isolation mothers experience when they are at home taking care of their children, but there is no direct confrontation with the complexities of the role itself. There is no acknowledgment that all the prejudices, myths, and ambiguities muddying the feminine role today are seen in their most bizarre glory in writings about mothers—especially in all those references to the "good" mother, the "normal" mother, the "adjusted" mother, and so forth. In fact, all the recent, rich analyses of the enculturation of women pay little in-depth attention to the two biggest assumptions about motherhood: the idea that a baby is woman's ultimate fulfillment and the evolution of sexually determined roles in bringing up children.

* Source Notes begin on page 151.

Though feminists have tolled the knell for the nuclear family, encouraged fathers to get involved in day-to-day child care, lamented the insular world that mothers have to offer their children, and applauded the advent of test-tube babies, motherhood still tends to be a subject avoided in the Women's Liberation Movement. The reasons for this are many. First of all, many feminist writers are not mothers, so they cannot talk about the role from firsthand experience. Being a mother is time consuming, so those who are in the best position to evaluate the role often do not have the opportunity to think and write. But the movement itself has a prejudice against mothers, perhaps even against thinking about their quandaries. Mothers are often treated as if they have "copped out," i.e., they have been found guilty of the ultimate in feminine behavior. Mothers are assumed to think along conservative lines because they have behaved traditionally in having a child, so their specific predicaments are ignored for the more obvious band-wagon issues. Our most militant, or at least articulate, sisters may also be afraid of scrutinizing woman's one status function, thereby making themselves more vulnerable than before. But the most important reason for the resounding silence on motherhood may be that most women have been sucked into the many mystifications surrounding every mention of maternity. All of us have internalized to some extent the propaganda that mothers should be blessed, all-good, all-understanding, all-generous, above petty passions, and, therefore, above scrutiny. It is easier to dream à la Germaine Greer of a magic farmhouse in southern Italy, worked by a kind local family, where you can rest and enjoy your children every month or so, than to figure out for yourself what changes need to be made in our thinking about motherhood so that women can develop in the role of mother.[2]

"Mystique" is an especially appropriate word for describing society's views on motherhood because the literature abounds with allusions to the enigmatic pregnant woman (e.g., the Mona Lisa), to religious fertility rites, to womb symbolism, and to communion with nature. Mothers are described as saints, because reproduction is equated with divine creation; then, in a complete reversal, mothers become the incarnation of mysterious evil, because dried-up blood (menstruation) is a frightening but necessary part of their life cycle. Womanliness is said to equal motherhood; nature is described as sending women into the world solely to be mothers and love children; and the "maternal instinct" is raised to the status of a governing passion. Napoleon's comment that women are machines for manufacturing children is not all that different from the prevailing belief that women are biologically programmed to be concerned first and foremost with child care.[3]

The myth that women exist only for motherhood is all around us. Pick up Mike Royko's best seller and see what he says about Mayor Daley:

He had those things that would be important to any man at sixty-eight, regardless of whether he was a mayor or a miner. His health was good, his hand steady. With his help, his sons were marching in his footsteps toward their own careers in law and politics. *His daughters had married and brought him grandchildren.*[4] (Emphasis added.)

Read a neurosurgery textbook, and you find this about a female patient: "Does she use her symptoms . . . to escape the day's work that a wife and mother should give to the service of others?"[5] Instead of questioning why she might *want* to "escape," we all have assumptions about what is proper feminine behavior, and these assumptions are reinforced daily without our even consciously thinking about them.

The "motherhood mystique" is conspicuous not only when people actually say a woman's function is to be a mother and to care for her children, but also in how unfeeling people are about the burden of motherhood. A crazy logic prevails, which maintains that since women are mothers, they can and want to do everything mothers are supposed to do. A. Alvarez's book, *The Savage God*, begins with a moving sketch of the author's relationship with Sylvia Plath in the years before her suicide. He relates the facts: in a little over two years, she gave birth to two children, had a miscarriage and an appendectomy, and was separated from her husband. Though he marvels at her poetic productivity during this period of intense physical stress and takes note of the fact that "the birth of her children . . . seemed to vindicate her as a woman,"[6] he seems oblivious to the emotional drain a sensitive new mother inevitably feels in shouldering the numerous pressures of the role itself. Even his phraseology betrays his own prejudices about what it means to be a mother; one wonders just how depressed Sylvia Plath felt on those days when she saw herself as anything *but* "vindicated as a woman."

Alvarez says that she had a "drab domestic life," was "efficient, bustling, harassed like every other housewife," but was "coping exceptionally well" and had "immersed herself in her children."[7] He even says that she saw herself as a Jewish mother,[8] but he presumes it was the desire to be reunited with her dead father, poetic necessity, and the London cold that were the precipitating factors in her death. Instead of telling us she was always available to her children (as if this were a proof of health), couldn't he just as well have described her death as at least indirectly due to the overwhelming burden she had to assume in acting out society's view of the always available mother? Maybe Sylvia Plath committed suicide a few hours before an *au pair* girl was to come and help her with the children and housework because she felt that getting domestic help was some final admission of failure as a coping woman? Alvarez seems aware of some of the tensions that she felt in being a "good mother"—he takes pains to tell us she left a plate of bread and butter and two mugs of milk in the children's room for their breakfast before she put her head in the gas oven—yet these tensions are dismissed as "normal" when he is drawing a picture of her. Why this invisible suffering?

The frustrations, anxieties, and dilemmas of being a mother are principally due to the notion that a baby is supposed to be woman's ultimate fulfillment and to the evolution of sex-determined functional roles in child rearing, two concepts that stifle the growth and development of all mothers. At first glance, fulfillment seems to have so many positive connotations; it promises serenity, satisfaction, even erotic gratification. There are psychiatric books that use the word "fulfillment" every time they refer to motherhood; each page practically shouts out the promise of pleasure. Let me quote Dr. Theodore Lidz, a noted psychiatrist, at some length to illustrate the existing social mythology:

Particularly for a wife, a sense of *fulfillment only comes* with the creation of a new life. Her biological purpose seems to *require completion* through conceiving, bearing, and nurturing children, and strong cultural and educational directives have added impetus to *this drive. Feelings of incompletion and deprivation in being a girl have been compensated* by realization of her innate capacities for creativity, but the realization requires actualization. Childhood fantasies of displacing mother and providing a child for father are now symbolically realized. The birth of a child *turns her into a woman* by setting her on a par with her mother. Her love for the husband *who has made such completion possible* deepens. She does not wish the child just for herself but as a meaningful outcome of her relatedness to her husband, *pleasing him with a gift* that is part of him that he has placed in her to nurture but also something of herself that the husband will cherish. To some extent, the baby is herself loved by a benevolent father.[9] (Emphases mine.)

A careful analysis of this passage suggests: (1) women experience their ultimate fulfillment only when pregnant; (2) woman is trapped in girlhood until she is pregnant; (3) girls feel incomplete and deprived, and the only cure is having a baby; (4) every married uterus should be used at least once; (5) women can please their husbands by giving gifts, and children are presents; (6) women are grateful to men for impregnating them; (7) if you want to be cherished, have a baby so your husband can see himself in miniature; he may also like you better if he sees you in miniature form. None of these sentiments sounds particularly appealing. They do not seem likely to encourage mental health. Babies do not cure anything; they are not presents. You can be a mature woman and never have a child; you can have two children and feel more like a shrew than a creative woman. The biological sense of the words—creativity, fulfillment, completion—are regularly confused with the psychological meanings, and the results are absolutely ludicrous. Pity the poor woman who can hope to be creative only by having a baby, who can find fulfillment only in opening wide her thighs for the sperm to go in and for the baby to come out. "Parenting" over the ensuing eighteen years can be a tremendously creative process, but for women the emphasis is usually on the procreative process alone. No one requires that a man copulate every four hours or whenever he is capable of an erection in order to fulfill his "biological purpose."

Closer analysis of the word "fulfill" suggests that men may want to "fill up" a woman more than she wants to be "full." The pleasant connotations of the term disappear when you ponder dictionary definitions that describe "fulfill" as doing the required, carrying out the expected, bringing to an end.[10] If to fulfill oneself is synonymous with completely realizing one's potentialities, then it is no wonder that women experience after-birth depression. After you have done the required and realized your ambitions, what is left? Baby as ultimate fulfillment comes to mean that you have very limited possibilities for satisfaction once past childbearing. Obviously this makes women expect much more from the experience of being a mother than they can ever reasonably get from their children. "Fulfillment" seems a poor substitute for a life that is full.

Since the civil rights movement of the sixties which sensitized us to the fallacies of "separate but equal" rhetoric, it is difficult to believe that many women would agree with psychoanalysts like Clara Thompson, who said,

. . . if in return for being a man's property a woman receives economic security, a full emotional life centering around husband and children, and an opportunity to express her capacities in the management of her home, she has little cause for discontent. The question of her inferiority scarcely troubles her when her life is happily fulfilled, even though she lives in relative slavery.[11]

Nevertheless, the mass media continue to blare out this propaganda with little understanding that a full emotional life and slavery are mutually exclusive terms. As Una Stannard says, "Modern men are saying what medieval theologians used to imply when they debated such questions as: 'Is not woman a higher type of animal put on earth like other animals for man's use?' "[12]

Men are not viewed as completely fulfilled until they reach old age and have many diverse experiences and accomplishments behind them, yet women are thought to find their greatest fulfillment in the vicarious thrill of producing a male child.[13] Alvarez found Sylvia Plath "made solid and complete, her own woman again," after the birth of her son, and he wondered if that wasn't the reason for "this new, confident air."[14] Yet the irony is that the mother is not her own woman; she is usually chained to the child under the guise of being the *selfless* nurturer. Like the Mother of God, "divinity is no longer her own, but depends on her motherhood . . . power and weakness meet and the necessary mother is dependent for her sacredness on her son."[15] A woman grows to physical maturity tantalized by the notion of becoming a smug fertility goddess, yet she is frightened by the inhumanity of being on a pedestal.

Outrageous expectations for what a woman should feel and be do not end with pregnancy and birth. Far from it. Women are held almost completely responsible for the rearing of children. Here is a fable that illustrates how sexual roles have been shaped by a preposterous emphasis on specialization. At some point, when the volcanic mists and vapors were rolling back to show an earth primed for fertility, someone had the ingenious idea that more could be accomplished if work was divided up by talent, age, and sex. Because, from the moment of birth, sex is the first obvious human difference, it probably took precedence over talent or age as definer of function. Men opted for hunting and fishing and some farming; women were assigned (note the cultural inclination to make them passive even in spinning a fable) the tasks of berry picking, wiping running noses, keeping the fires going, and other domestic chores. Specialization worked out fairly well and caught on.

Millennia went by. Medicine, physics, chemistry, economics, philosophy, sociology, psychology, and psychiatry came into being and made the world more complicated. There were new tasks to master and divvy up. Everyone assumed that the more you knew about the different parts of life, the better you could understand the whole. Doctors began to specialize only in the care of the left index finger. Chemical industries devoted to exterminating only the gypsy moth took their place in society, and a government agency committed to burning the poppy fields in the northeastern sector of the western part of Turkey got funded for the next ninety-nine years. Back at the hearth, berry picking was turned over to berry pickers, fires were left to firemen, running noses were given over to vitamin C salesmen. So that the sexes could continue to tell each other apart, social scientists talked about descriptions of functional roles in the family.

Here is one example of how things have come to be divided in modern times. "Father's primary goal may be to support his family; mother's may be not only to keep everybody fed, clothed, and looked after but, hopefully, *to keep everybody happy*."[16] (Emphasis mine.) Using bigger words to describe some of the same things, the sociologist Morris Zelditch, Jr., says that because "the female is allocated the integrative-supportive role, there must necessarily be an allocation of authority for discipline and relatively 'neutral' judgment to the husband-father . . . the male adult will play the role of instrumental leader and the female adult will play the role of expressive leader."[17] Instrumental leader means that the man makes the money, gets prestige for the family in the community, and protects the child from the mother's emotional excesses. Expressive leader means that the woman makes everybody happy. We are either this or that; apparently, familial matters go better if tasks are done in pieces. Presumably, life is more perfect if the woman is the heart and the man is the head of the family. How could a family with two adult hearts and two adult heads function? If we aren't careful, bodily organs may atrophy with cultural disuse for the good of society.

This fable about the evolution of sex-determined functional roles should leave you wondering whether it is necessary to divide up parent roles, and the heavyhanded irony about mind/heart metaphors—an old-time favorite in marriage services—should have you questioning whether you have any chance of developing children with integrated personalities when the parents are so top-heavy (or bosom-heavy, as the case may be) in their own development. What kind of a world do we live in when we distinguish between a mother's loving the child and a father's encouraging independence?[18] How narrow are we when fathers are warned not to get too involved in diapering or feeding their children because the baby may end up with two mothers?[19] Are we talking about mothers or monsters when we say that "some significant member of the nuclear family must 'pry the child loose' from its mother-dependency so that it may 'grow up' and accept its responsibilities as an 'adult?' "[20] Aren't mothers "significant?" In a very insidious way, emotions have come to be associated with being a child, something you grow out of with the help of Father. There is a presumption that mothers function at a *lower,* more juvenile and hysterical level than fathers, who are assumed to have better control over their behavior. The mind of one person is supposed to direct the heart of another. Can't the expressive mother be rational, too? Have we gone so far into a climate of fragmentation and stereotype that we cannot think in terms of a mother who can comfort bumped heads *and* urge her child to take her/his junior year of college abroad to see more of the world? Can't a mother be both self-sacrificing and demanding, nurturing yet able to encourage independence in the child? Is there no mother who can make "a relatively neutral judgment?"

If women in general have been typed as emotional puffs of prettiness, it is obvious that mothers have even more of a problem with stereotype. They are encouraged to be one-sided; then they are held accountable for not raising "whole" children. They are told to be the expressive members of the family, yet they are blamed when the father is withdrawn, reserved, and unable to express affection.[21] Who wouldn't opt for an eight-hour or even a fourteen-hour job in some office or factory, rather than feel responsible on a round-the-clock basis for keeping the whole family "happy"? Talk about impossible jobs! The new mother may just be getting used to her own mood swings when suddenly there are distinguished authorities telling her she is totally responsible for the emotional climate in her sweet, little, mortgaged home. There are days when it seems that being a mother is to be the all-time scapegoat. Fulfillment, snarl! And, remember, the mother is not only responsible for the happiness of her children but is expected to keep her husband happy (he apparently grew up without the capacity to do that for himself). As Dr. Joyce Brothers puts it:

It all adds up to offering your husband only your best self. Forgo the luxury of indulging in moods of irritability, discontent, and envy. These are luxuries. It means one more strike against you in your effort to keep the irreplaceable treasure—your husband's romantic love. . . . Your problem is to be sure you remain a woman, just as alluring, feminine and interesting to your husband as before the advent of the child. That, in addition to your responsibilities as a mother, will give you a very, very fulltime job.[22]

Women may not have their heads screwed on, but they can still smell garbage when it is all around them. Mothers are not simply attractive vestal virgins who happen to have cute children curled up near the fireplace. How can you be an interesting person and not have moods?

Not only is it an insult to men's self-esteem to say that women are the ones who act as the "guardians of emotion and the guides to its expression,"[23] but this kind of thinking places horrible and thoroughly impossible pressures on all mothers. In the opinion of many mental-health professionals, the mother is a failure if the family is unhappy. It is not surprising that mothers have tended to be indulgent with their children or become confused about how they should handle the various growth and development crises. A "good" guardian of emotion should think in terms of long-range character goals, but it is very easy to take one's assignment literally and never frustrate anyone's wishes or desires by imposing limits. Why opt for more complicated thinking if you aren't supposed to be able to make a "relatively neutral judgment"? Excesses in the role of expressive leader occur easily if social mythology equates emotions with being emotional, without considering the fact that *the emotions are always part of any full human response to a situation.* The burden of being responsible for everyone's happiness is enormous and produces an army of frustrated, unhappy mothers. And the myth is perpetuated that happiness is bestowed in childhood by a placid mother-fairy rather than developed through a lifetime of hard work in coming to terms with your own problems and possibilities.

All the existing role distinctions between the sexes are based on the assumption that the genitals determine who should do what. Women have the babies; that is a fact. But it is also a biological fact that half the baby's chromosomes come to her or him thanks to the father. This suggests to me that while the mother has a unique role for ten lunar months, from the moment the baby is born it should be a shared pleasure and responsibility. And there should be a variety of ways for each parent to meet this responsibility. But more about options later.

Because a woman has functioning mammary glands, it does not logically follow that she should forever be responsible for the nurturing needs (or the cooking, for that matter) of the entire family. Just because the man can flood the woman's womb with a fertile spray does not mean that he has to be the gardener of the family or be forever responsible for fertilizing the minds of his children. There is something both dangerous and ridiculous about inferring social norms from physiological functioning. What does the shape of a woman's breasts have to do with mountain-climbing expertise? Having testicles does not prepare a man for being the reservoir of all wisdom. Both sexes have emerged from the last ten thousand years with certain inclinations, but these were probably more determined by cultural pressures than by anatomical distinctions. Women are described as docile, understanding, patient, passive, intuitive, and sympathetic. They are supposed to be more alert to the subtleties of personal relationships and to shades of feeling in human experience.[24] But did breasts, a vagina, ovaries, and a uterus encourage this?

A girl grows up believing she should develop a well-rounded personality, but she soon finds out that this doesn't mean the same thing for her as it does for boys; well-rounded females have curves, not character. She is told that her personal goals and public education should be oriented to being a wife and mother, since these roles are her destiny.* It's the old dichotomy: men are encouraged to change the world; women are expected to have relationships. Even authors who approve of liberating both men and women from constraining stereotypes subtly call into question the merits of egalitarian relationships between the sexes when they say "each sex still has a different set of missions; each marches to a slightly different piper."[25] Relationships are important. The relationship between mother and child can be a beautiful experience for both generations, but unrealistic social expectations and an unrelenting sense of total responsibility have marred this role for many.

In her book *Man's World, Woman's Place*, Elizabeth Janeway sums up the "motherhood mystique" that limits our ability to help our children grow and develop, as well as a woman's possibilities for personal maturity:

We must conclude that our society today is asking women to bring off something of an emotional *tour de force*. First, they are asked to regard the bearing and raising of children as at least a very large and significant

---

* Since Dr. Haim Ginott's book, *Between Parent and Child*, takes such a biological determination stand on male/female roles, I had intended to quote him here at some length in order to criticize his point of view. Unfortunately, I was refused permission to quote the relevant passages in Chapter Ten.

concern of their lives and, perhaps, as the crown and center of their existence, although, in the nature of things, this undertaking will demand their full efforts for something less than two decades out of a life that will run to seventy years. Second, they must fit their children for a society whose needs and aims are at best uncertain, and which may in fact seem to the mothers as well as the children morally unjustified and emotionally unsatisfying. At the same time, the most admired goals of society are pretty well closed to these women themselves. Third, they are expected to do all this only by means of an emotional relationship, instead of (as in the past) with the help of economic activities and social processes that relate to the larger world. . . . Fourth, having called forth this relationship, mothers are aware that they should maintain it in such a delicate balance that the child can grow out of it without harm to his own psychic strength. This program they are supposed to carry out with little training and little support from society itself, in the belief that any failure will justly be laid at their door.[26]

Given Ms. Janeway's crisp analysis, one wonders how it is ever possible for the mother to meet the demands that this role brings. No wonder men hesitate to become "second mothers"; they naturally do not want to have a nervous breakdown. According to one authority, the developmental tasks of the new mother include: reconciling conflicting conceptions of roles; accepting and adjusting to the strains and pressures of young motherhood; learning how to care for her infant with competence and assurance; providing full opportunities for the child's development; making satisfactory adjustments to the practical realities of life; keeping alive some sense of personal autonomy through young motherhood. There are also four other items, plus subtasks too numerous to list.[27] Is it any wonder that social scientists have been able to prove statistically that child rearing is related to "a high level of negative feelings" in the mother?[28] One wonders what took them so long to arrive at that brilliant conclusion.

What can we do about the situation? In listing some of the predicaments and pious drivel that mothers directly encounter in both serious and popular literature, we have taken the first step toward solution. It is not wishful thinking to say that you have to know a problem exists before you can do anything about it. Consciousness-raising is essential for growth and development; that is what psychiatry is all about. Mothers will feel less like emotional pawns when they start questioning existing social mythology.

We need to start thinking about the double-edged effect of statements like "Nature intended you to have children, and you are endowed with a natural capacity for motherhood."[29] Mystical allusions confuse instead of illuminate. The assumption that women act by instinct reinforces the notion that they are somehow not rational, or it suggests that they function on a more primitive level than men do. If you do not feel anything like a "natural capacity for motherhood," you may start wondering if you are a normal woman or if you have missed out on learning something every other woman knows. Yes, women are the ones who get pregnant, but what does it mean to act by instinct?

What are the social, political, and economic reasons that conspire to keep women out of the community-at-large? Is it paranoid to think that commercial interests have a stake in maintaining present mystifications? I don't think so. If bearing a child raises your social status, how will you feel when no one listens to you, even when you are a mother? Do you want to live your own life or to live vicariously?

We must raise questions, all sorts of delicious, evil, naughty, important questions. Why is there a "motherhood mystique?" Why do men want to describe their women as weak? Is it because they are still shocked by the power their mothers demonstrated in giving them life? Why do women see themselves as psychoanalytic scapegoats and do nothing about it? Why? Why? Why? Learning how to phrase the questions is part of the answer to the problem. Questioning is part of coping; it is the precursor to being capable of making a "relatively neutral judgment." Not to question is to act blindly, and then we are "destined" to be frustrated. We need to get into the habit of not assuming that *descriptions* of existing behavior necessarily have any relation to *prescriptions* for behavior. Just because a woman has a uterus does not mean that filling up punch bowls is an *inherently* feminine activity.

We cannot change mores and myths until we first understand ourselves. If you become aware that many of your unreasonable actions and reactions are fashioned more by social convention than by your own judgment, you are better able to deal with the crazy aspects of role pressures. Every woman needs to understand the binds that the motherhood mystique puts her in so she will be more able to question her own responses in a given situation. For example, if you begin to wonder why society thinks bearing babies is fulfilling, you may be able to understand why you got so mad at that two-week bundle of fulfillment when she or he screamed for fifteen minutes for no apparent reason. Are you angry partly because you are projecting expectations on the baby that no baby could possibly meet? Obviously, you are reacting to the baby's behavior, but you are also reacting to the fact that the baby is not making you feel good or "fulfilled" in the way you hoped and were led to expect. Maybe this insight will make you feel less angry at the baby, because the baby is not to blame for your disappointment. And maybe you will be appropriately skeptical when you pick up the next child-care pamphlet.

It is the mother's obligation to acquaint herself with the conscious and unconscious pressures hounding her on all sides. Not only for her own sake but also to safeguard her child from harm of the most insidious kind, which results when she makes demands the child can hardly be expected to meet. A good place to start for the woman interested in growing and developing as a mother is to ask herself honestly, "Why did I have this baby?" "What did I think a baby would do for me?" "Never mind what society says it should mean; what does it actually mean to me?"

Of course, parents don't have children because they want to be martyrs, or at least they shouldn't. They have them because they love children and want some of their very own. They also love children because they remember being loved so much by their parents in their childhood. Taking care of their children, seeing them grow and develop into fine people, gives most parents—despite the hard work—their greatest satisfaction in life.

—*Dr. Benjamin Spock*[1]

2

Why Have Babies?

Why did I have a baby? So that my life would be "fuller," my personal world would be more "complete," and I would feel more "satisfied." I wanted to be happy. I longed to have one "perfect" relationship with another human being, a relationship unmarred by pettiness and in which I would be completely accepted and loved for myself. I wanted to get back to nature, to feel more feminine, to see if being pregnant would make me look prettier and softer. I was a product of the "motherhood mystique." Everything I yearned for had more to do with my own pleasure than with wanting to love and care for a real baby. My feelings were not unusual, but these romantic fictions were anything but conducive to dealing with the practicalities of being a parent.

How many people have babies simply and solely "because they love children?" Very few indeed, I suspect. Even when children are wanted and planned for (something that is not as common as one might think, even among those who are sophisticated about birth control), people have babies for all sorts of reasons that have absolutely nothing to do with loving children. If you start believing the saccharine propaganda that normal women have babies because they love children, you may be knee-deep in guilt before the doctor confirms you are pregnant. There you are, barely pregnant, and already depressed because you aren't the ideal mother. Instead of smiling at this further proof of the basic ambivalence of all relationships, you may start chastizing yourself and your husband for having impure motives. You will probably do a good job of intimidating yourself. And if you avoid thinking about why you did decide to have a baby and what the waiting period really means to you, this may minimize your chances for becoming comfortable in the new role. Guilty and ashamed, you will miss the fun of contemplating a new adventure. You may even set up a situation in which you will be inclined to resent the child when she or he arrives so unlovable. You know you "love children," so it must be the baby's fault if you find it hard to love her or him.

Why do women have babies? First of all, because it is *the* thing for a woman to do. If you don't have a child, friends start wondering whether you have a physical problem that prevents you from conceiving a baby, and they begin recommending fertility doctors. Relatives either start feeling sorry for you because you are "barren," or they start hinting that you are "too selfish" to have children. You begin to feel guilty that you are still "free," and you wonder if you really are inadequate and self-centered.

If you remember being loved by your parents, you probably want to have a child to find out what it feels like to be admired the way you admired your own parents. I think this is more likely than because you are dying to give love. Having a child may mean that you are finally emancipated from your own parents. Once I was pregnant, I expected them to see me as an equal, mature, no more their "flighty kid." Having a baby is a rite of transition. For a woman to be considered fully "grown up" in much of American society, she has to have children. If she wants people to listen to her as a responsible person, she has to be able to show her credentials—Tom, Ann, Billy, Wendy, and so forth.

I even remember looking forward to the time when I could complain, and could say, "That child is always on the go; I always have to be right behind her or she'll get into trouble. With all the running around I do, it's a wonder I'm not bone-thin." I grew up hearing variations on this theme, and I wanted an excuse to complain back. There was a crazy irresistible urge to forsake the pleasures of regular restaurant going for the chance to look long-suffering (discreetly, of course). I wanted some of the sympathy society reserves for mothers. I wanted to be able to go to a friend's home and respond in kind to any anecdotes I might hear about thumb sucking or the cost of shoes. I felt that without a child I was missing out on something. Mind you, I was repulsed by the image of parent as martyr, but the only way I could respond to "Boy, do you have it easy now; wait 'til you are tied down by kids" was to want shackles for myself.

Or maybe instead of being motivated by imitation or identification, you want to have a baby to prove to your parents and in-laws how much better a parent you are than they ever dreamed of being. You imagine a time when your mother-in-law tells you she is so pleased her first grandchild has your dimples and easy disposition. She confides how proud she is that her son had the good sense to marry you. In the next fantasy, your mother mentions how amazed she is you find time to bake your own bread, read everything on the best-seller list, do typing for your husband, and spend so much time with your children. What's more, she admits she never had the organizational skill, good humor, creative flair, energy, patience, understanding, pungent wit, quiet dignity, buoyant charm, cool-headed practicality, and kindliness you display.

While I do not want to discount the generosity implicit in deciding to take on the responsibilities of motherhood, I do want to make clear that fantasies, obsessions, ambivalent memories, and game playing are the emotional rule rather than the exception. Before I had a child of my own, I did not have the opportunity to know many children, much less to love them. Baby-sitting experiences were few and far between; children scared me. I always felt they were able to size me up better than I could myself (another myth). Even my younger cousins had grown up by the time I decided to take a close look at children. Instead of loving children, I grew up in love with the *idea* of loving children, just as I grew up in love with the idea of loving the "right" man. Somehow, I always hoped that the perfect husband would transform me into the perfect woman; children conceived out of perfect love would put me in harmony with myself, my friends, and family. (Variations on these themes are constantly preached to us by magazines, commercials, movies, and television.)

Oh, I knew from my observations of families that angry words and sullen moods were not banished by maternal kisses and conjugal love, but I was sure that these ultimate relationships would be so enriching to me that I could not help but feel happy and joyful most of the time. It would be *different* with me. Going away to college and having an apartment of my own—past turning points—had not squelched my tendency to mutter away the morning or eliminated my taste for butterscotch sundaes when I was depressed, but I was convinced that a husband who really loved me would transform me into a slender, patient, generous, even-tempered, loving woman. Well, I found marriage does not bring instant fulfillment, and it's not the magic route to self-improvement. You get used to the pleasures of having letters addressed "Mrs." and of gesturing with your beringed left hand very quickly. Cultivating my sexual appetite did not lessen my taste for chocolate cake. I soon began to question how perfect my husband was since he fell in love with imperfect me. Maybe he wasn't "Mr. Right" since I still had regular cycles of feeling depressed and mean. Where was the *complete fulfillment* that the ladies' magazines talked about?

I began to think more and more about the warm, soft, tactile world of childhood. Having a baby would be my chance for self-renewal. How wonderful it would be to unhook my bra and have the baby suck. I could feel those happy hormones tugging at my womb, confirming my lustiness, while I gave my husband a loving look, part earth mother, part Madonna. I would finally be a complete woman. My love affair with my child would be a pure, beautiful, holy relationship. Every day would brim over with bright colors and lullabies, cuddling and snuggling, balloons, and gurgling sounds. Oh, how we would sing and dance—even though I cannot carry a tune and am self-conscious about expressing the rhythm I feel. In my reverie, the waves would play hide-and-seek with my toes as I put the dandelion flag on the tower of the sand castle. My child and I would lazily comb the beach for seashell soldiers to guard the princess's home.

Before you start thinking I am terribly naïve, let me add that I am deliberately sketching a caricature of my feelings. Part of me understood that no mortal, man or child would ever make me feel completely contented and happy, for such "highs" can never be sustained in day-to-day living. I realized that ambivalence characterizes all relationships, but that did not stop me from indulging in a wild romanticism that I was barely aware of at the time. Only gradually did I realize that real self-fulfillment depends on coming to terms with these preposterous fictions that all of us devise, especially when we grow up encouraged to think that having a husband and children equals some sort of automatic happiness or fulfillment.

So much for explanation; now back to my castle building. In a way, I saw having a baby as my last chance to become one with nature, to come to terms with my own body. I have never enjoyed picnics, swimming, and other sports the way vibrant, alive people are supposed to. My legs constantly cramp when I am sitting yoga style on a blanket at a picnic; the ants get more of my attention than the trees and flowers do. I invariably cut my foot on a sharp seashell when I am at the beach, and seaweed regularly ensnares my ankles. I like the sun but hate sweating. I enjoy watching a graceful tennis return but never seem to forget my bobbing derriere when I am returning a serve. These confessions of a girl scout dropout may not seem to have much in common with having babies, but babies mean trees, flowers, picnics, and ball playing to me. Somehow, I felt that watching my baby at a picnic or on the beach or climbing on a jungle gym would diminish my own clumsiness. A body that could produce something beautiful must have some beauty itself.

I wanted to have a baby because I was tired of working. My job was difficult, and I needed some time out to figure where I wanted to go in my profession. Having a baby is the perfect out. Who would ever think you were having a baby to figure out who you were and where you were going? I wanted to get away from the pressures of committee meetings, student evaluations, correcting papers, feeling inadequate as a nurse-teacher. Why get too enmeshed in a career when you know that there will come a time when you "have to" have a baby because all married people eventually do that sort of thing? I was tired of feeling capable and thinking about patient welfare. What about my own welfare? My husband took good care of me; I did not have to worry about balancing the checkbook at the end of the month and overseeing the care of the car. How lovely it would be to be pregnant and have everyone be solicitous about me.

It would be a splendid adventure, a grand experiment. Put my genes and my husband's chromosomes together, and what do you get? Will he be handsome? Will she be pretty? Oh, how desperately I wanted to have a beautiful child.

Our parents were beginning to hint that we should give them their first grandchild. What a pleasure to have them engrossed in the next generation and leave us alone in that land of indifference that grown-up children go to once they have offspring of their own. I was sure there would be no more strains and disagreements once we all had something in common to talk about: how precocious the baby is.

How lovely to go to a party and have an answer to that question, "And how many children do you have?"

Will I be able to get pregnant? I wonder how long it will take? Better have a child before I am so old people will laugh at me crossing the street with a baby carriage. I wonder if my husband will love me more if I "give" him a child? He would never think of divorcing me if we had children. They say breast feeding can be a very sexual experience; I wonder how I'll feel.

If I have a baby, I will never feel lonely again.

I wonder how much it hurts?

With all these thoughts and feelings, and many more unremembered, I became pregnant. Somehow, it was a shock to my view of myself as a "fertile Myrtle" not to become pregnant the first month we tried.

Doubts and worries crowded in. But they were nothing compared with the ambivalent hodgepodge of feelings that pregnancy itself brought. I began to think ambivalence might be my middle name. By ambivalence, I mean real love and real hate at one and the same time, not some watered-down neutral feelings. I had so many thoughts and feelings, but I was able to name many of them only when I thought about them several years later. In hindsight, I realize I was constantly struggling with the motherhood mystique, with what I actually felt, and what I thought I should feel. A diary during those months might have read:

> *I have finally done it; I am elated and terrified. For the first time in my life, I feel like a woman. . . . What is happening to my body? I should be feeling joyful all the time, but I am nauseated and tired all the time. I am overwhelmed by the stirrings in my body. Will I ever recapture that friendly indifference I had before to my physical self? Will I ever have any energy again or am I already the beaten hausfrau? . . . I have always been intrigued by pseudocyesis (imagined pregnancy). Am I only imagining these changes because I want to have a baby so much? . . . And yet I definitely do not want to have a child: "Go away, I don't want you." Am I destined to balloon like the ill-fated Mary of England because I want an heir, because I want some stake in the future? I want to say "go away" and make the puffiness in my breasts and belly subside.*

Yes, I want this child; I hate my husband for making me pregnant. . . . No, I don't really hate him, but I want to hate him. How wonderful when women were raped and they could blame men for what happened. I chose to be pregnant. Why? How could any rational creature permit an outside force to take over her body? I want to be mad at someone, but who? . . . All those whispered stories about women dying in childbirth haunt me. Maybe I should have taken ballet classes as a girl, so my muscles would be more flexible. Why didn't I wait until I myself was in perfect health? I want to vomit and vomit. I despise feeling green and purple all the time, yet I enjoy making loud, disgusting retching sounds in the bathroom so my husband feels worried and guilty. . . . I'm just a pawn in the generation game.

I just had a dream that was all sensation. I stroked the baby's fuzzy cherub head and smooth yielding body. My hand melted into the velvety warmth of the baby; I felt so peaceful.

Why were our parents less than ecstatic when we announced that they would become grandparents in June? I wish my father would shut up and stop reminding me that we should start saving money now that we are expecting a child. Who the hell cares whether "it" gets to college? . . . I want to go out to dinner tonight and eat all sorts of salty things so I can swell up in style. . . . I really enjoyed telling my husband that I didn't want to make love tonight because I feel so lousy. I am locked into a game with him that I don't even know the name of.

I feel like a cow; I haven't gotten angry in weeks. I really am happy and contented. That satisfied smile must be driving some of my friends crazy with envy, or at least I hope it is. . . . For the first time in my life, I have an excuse for being plump. I am round and soft-looking. Yeah, no one expects me to be sylphlike. I am above competing with other women over who has the sexiest figure. . . . It is embarrassing to have *everyone know that you have a sex life. I blush more these days when I meet men because I know that there is something very vulgar about me. Vulgar grandeur, that's what I feel. . . . It is a dream, and things will return to normal soon, I hope.*

I am frightened by the fact that my mother-in-law just asked me if I would like a subscription to Reader's Digest *for my birthday now that I will be home with a baby. Is she trying to tell me that I will not have the time, or maybe the inclination, to read whole books once I am a mother? My mother gave me a ten-year subscription to one of the ladies' magazines for Christmas. She said that I will probably enjoy looking at fashions and recipes more, once I am no longer working. I like clothes and domestic things, but will I be imprisoned in a world of ruffled gingham and nursery rhymes and salmon mousse?*

My husband greets me every evening with "How are you and the blob today?" The "blob" bounces around a good deal now. I am so proud of those strong kicks. Does the baby feel comforted in that steamy, dark web when I stroke my massive stomach? . . . I dreamed that my stomach stretched and stretched and stretched, and I had to keep eating and eating so my body would not feel empty and lonely. I keep wanting to eat and eat to reaffirm myself and the baby. . . . We went out to a big family dinner. How wonderful not to feel that you have to offer to wash the dishes. . . . Old ladies now smile at me when I go to the grocery store and ask me if it is my first. . . . I am so damned unwieldy. . . . My husband is indulging me; he even tolerates my taste for murder mysteries without snickering.

I just dreamed that the child was born without any hands and feet, and it refused to die. Everyone expects me to take good care of the monster because I am a nurse. I hate it; I hate it; I hate it. I refuse to be chained to this house forever.

Why do people keep reminding us that the baby will force us to change our life style, "to settle down." Who wants to be settled? It sounds like death. Why the gloating comments? It sounds as if we are being punished for having a sex life.

One person tells me that birth pains are just like severe menstrual cramps; others tell of twenty-four, forty-eight hours of horror. What is the truth? . . . I have gone to the childbirth classes and practiced the breathing exercises, but I still cannot convince myself that I will ever need to use them. My husband and I saw the movie at one of those classes in which you can see the baby edge his head out. I could not look. My bottom began to throb at the thought of that kind of abuse. I am disgusting. . . . I feel under siege; the final assault is imminent. Will I die? Maybe I will die because I did not conceive a child for the right motives. My seed will be cursed because of my sins.

I do not ever want to stop being pregnant. My body enjoys a speeded-up metabolism. My pores have closed up, and my complexion is really rosy. I like to rest my hands on the jumping mound. I like to pat my stomach. I feel arrogant and wanton. . . . I am now too pregnant for sex. I feel virginal, precious. I am initiated into the sisterhood. . . . Who would have ever thought my whims would be accorded such importance? I have only to look a little winded, and my husband does whatever I asked him to do. This is the first time in my life I've ever felt delicate or fragile. I never want to stop feeling precious, and yet I keep pretending to be casual about it all.

Tombstones that read "Beloved Mother of _____" have always fascinated me. At last, I am going to be someone's beloved mother. Will I love the baby and be loved in return? The thought that my baby might not love me scares me.

I dreamed that all three of us rolled over and over in a field of daisies.

I want a boy first because I always wanted to have an older brother. Can I bear it if it is a girl? I hate a world that places such importance on the first-born being a boy. Why can't you feel equally fulfilled with a girl? . . . I want a little boy so I can stare at his penis without interruption. I am a sex fiend for even thinking of how much I will enjoy looking at my boy's genitals and admiring his sexuality. I am going to be punished for my thoughts and feelings; the baby will be born a hermaphrodite.

I used to enjoy complaining about my girth; I am now too big to even enjoy it. I can't sleep at night. Where will I ever get the energy to take care of this child? I am a slave. . . . I feel like a rosebush, rooted in the ground and doomed to bud. . . . Finally, I screwed up enough courage to buy some baby things. I do not want to have many things in the house in case the baby dies. If something happens to the baby, I will never be able to look at a baby again without crying. . . . I keep wanting to make deals with God. If I send money to missionaries and swear to think only proper thoughts, will He give me a perfect child?

It is so important to me to have a beautiful baby. Can I be loving to a child with a big nose, floppy ears, and a weak chin?

I keep thinking over and over again about what I would do if my child and I were drowning, and only one of us could be saved. Good mothers are supposed to put the child's welfare ahead of their own without any hesitation. I hope the situation never comes up. I don't know what I would do. Maybe I'll give him swimming lessons at six months.

It is not worth all of this just to get presents on Mother's Day.

I am now a week overdue. The doctor assures me this regularly happens the first time, but I am convinced the baby will never come out. Maybe he will get bigger and bigger and bigger, and will eventually burst out leaving behind a pool of protoplasm that used to be me.

I hate being known as Bill's wife; now I am destined to go through life being so-and-so's mother. I am a "has-been" even before I have ever been a "been."

Will I ever really have a baby of my very own to hug and kiss and cuddle in my arms?

I can understand the novel *Rosemary's Baby* as never before. All mothers must have vague feelings that some devil planted a baby inside of them for his own nasty purposes. There is an evil divinity in me. I feel like the blackest of Madonnas— mean, spiteful, murderous. . . . I feel blessed by something beyond me, for I now have a stake in history. This is my second chance for perfection. I am now connected to all the other people on this planet who have ever had babies. I understand why you do not want to die without a portion of yourself continuing on and on, yet sometimes I wonder if I am not more suited to being a grandmother than to being a mother. I can imagine myself taking care of children for three or four days, but not all the time.

I love this baby fiercely, and yet I do not know whether I will even like him when we first meet. . . . This baby is my masterpiece, my creation, my work of art. Our child will be the proof of the love my husband and I have for each other. But suppose the baby is sickly? Does that mean that our love is also less than perfect? . . . I find myself being less judgmental when I am with friends who have children. I won't blame them for the obnoxious behavior of their children so they won't blame me for the bad humor of my own.

Even though the contractions have started and I am about to come face to face with the friendly parasite, I dread the meeting. I am going to have to stop playing the role of the radiant

*pregnant woman and become the capable mother. I like be-
ing pregnant, but will I like being a mother? My body craves
release, yet I feel uneasy, the way you do when you are being
interviewed for your first job. . . . I am so excited and
thrilled.*

This chaotic medley of thoughts and feelings—some grand and
some petty—surely proves Simone de Beauvoir's statement that
"maternity is usually a strange mixture of narcissism, altruism, idle
daydreaming, sincerity, bad faith, devotion, and cynicism."[2] And I
do not think that the intense adrenalin-filled muddle that I have
attributed to the decision to have babies and the nine-month wait is
confined to the first pregnancy. Parents never have children just
because "they love children and want some of their very own."
Wanting to put a child between yourself and different relationships and pressures, wanting to prove your own worth (your own
fertility, creativity, sexuality, and sensuality), and wanting to fight
off loneliness are important considerations in all pregnancies.
Having babies is identified with being loved, beautiful, youthful,
and natural, so these pulls are bound to exert a strong influence in
any decision to enlarge one's family. The more you understand
these pressures, the more you will be able to handle your feelings,
so they do not intrude in an unhealthy way on your relationship
with your child.

There are all sorts of added notions and emotions that do pop
up the second time. In subsequent pregnancies, the sex of the baby
usually becomes very important. A woman who has already had a
girl and believes in Zero Population Growth, can be a desperate
woman during her second wait. This is her last chance to have a
boy. It is the last chance for her husband to feel that he "was man
enough to produce a son." Her husband and daughter may already
have a special, ardent relationship and this is her last chance to
have a "partner" in the family. The competition between mother
and daughter can get awfully strong for the attentions of the

father, and it is the most normal feeling in the world to want someone on your side.

During the second pregnancy, you may have serious doubts about whether you can love the new child as much as you loved the first one, or you may desperately hope that the new relationship will be more cordial this time around. One thing I have observed in myself and many of my friends is that the mother becomes obsessed in the second pregnancy with the idea that she is having the baby for the child who is already there. I remember thinking that I "owed" it to my daughter to supply her with a playmate who would not have to go home at suppertime. Everyone does a good job of making you feel this is the appropriate thing to do. There are strong hints in the child-rearing books that your child will be lonely if a sibling is not provided, or even more damning, that she will turn into a "spoiled brat." Childhood memories are reactivated. If you had a younger sister, as I did, you begin to remember how much you resented your sister's arrival, and you can become very worried that the same family pattern will repeat itself, because you imagine you will always side with your older daughter. You begin to feel guilty about wanting your children to be three years apart—so one will be out of diapers, instead of wanting them to be eighteen months apart so "they can play together." *The fantasy that perfection is possible hounds you.* If there were two boys and two girls in your family, you may think that is the ideal combination, and any other blend is doomed to failure. You begin to evolve some notion of what the sex balance in a family should be, what the number balance should be, and what optimal spacing is. You keep hoping for the right mixture that will *guarantee* that all members of the family will get along with each other.

The male-female struggle that influenced some of the fantasies of the first pregnancy come back with renewed vigor: "your" baby, "my" baby, "our" baby. One can experience a tremendous sorrow if this is the last child you intend to have. You become preoccupied

with the thought that this may be your last chance to find fulfillment. Can old age be far behind? Who wants to feel that her
"youth" and "productive" years are behind her? Even if you
despise diapers, you may not want to give up complaining about
them. If you have a loud, busy household, it may prove tempting
to have a baby to get out of work and stop being so capable. Not
that most women really do get out of work, but they have more
opportunity to bemoan their situation when they are pregnant. It is
so much more acceptable to complain about your unwieldy bulk
than to confess that taking care of the children who are already
there overwhelms you. It is easy to ignore how much of a burden
the baby will be over the next eighteen years when you yearn for
nine months of special worth if only in the eyes of your obstetri-
cian and your husband. Mixed motives and mixed emotions are
clearly not limited to the first pregnancy.

There are some authorities who talk and write in terms of "the
more childish and timid wife" who will feel this way, "the already
mature independent woman" who will feel this way, and "women
who are most concerned with themselves" will feel yet another
way, and so on. We should be warned against this kind of labeling
and categorizing of behavior. It is a mistake to talk about one kind
of woman responding in a certain way at a certain point in her life.
Such packaging of behavior presupposes that there is an "appropriate" response for every individual, but human emotions are
never neat and are rarely appropriate. Every woman has babies for
all sorts of reasons, conscious and unconscious. During pregnancy
and childbirth, every woman is bound to feel a little of everything:
dependent and independent, passive and rebellious, contented and
tense, sulky and serene, stoic and complaining, submissive and
domineering. This is not the same as saying that one's emotions are
labile during this period, *i.e.,* that one experiences mood swings.
But such a profound experience is bound to force each individual
to think and feel a multitude of things; *this is normal.*

Having a baby is a physiological and psychological turning
point. Your notion of bodily integrity is violated in a much more

dramatic fashion than the advent of the first menses or the first act
of intercourse. Even if you are not susceptible to the usual discom-
forts of pregnancy (ankle swelling, sore breasts, nausea, vomiting,
fatigue, heartburn, feeling bloated, forgetting where you begin
and end), you are bound to feel at times that your body has been
possessed and that you have lost control of your own person. You
can view it as a violent siege, an opportunity for physical transcendence, a chance to see if your body functions properly, or a slight
inconvenience—well worth the price—but pleasure and pain will
always go hand in hand, and ambivalence is the only correct, the
only possible emotional posture. Every transition brings its share
of fears (real dangers and specific problems) and anxieties (a
diffuse sense of danger, unspecific tension), and they are in
abundance when you are having a baby, which calls for a whole
new life style. Your entire life up until this point has been self-
centered, and reasonably so, because you have been trying to figure
out who you are in relation to the rest of the world. You have
spent years trying to figure out whether you are pretty, whether you
are generous, whether you are smart, whether you are sexy,
whether you are personable, whether you are witty, gay, and
charming. Wondering if you will marry, wondering if you will
have a career have kept you awake nights, thinking.

It is ironic that courtship and the honeymoon, the most self-
centered periods of one's life, should be followed by having
babies, which demands a giving of self in a whole new way.
Finding a marital partner implies that one is interested enough in
other people to want to enter into a relationship with someone
else. But most of us are a bit like Narcissus in our search for the
"beloved"; we are looking for someone who will show us how
beautiful we are, who will validate the fact that we are desirable.
We can love the other one because his own talents reflect our good
taste. The spouse's position, background, charm, and physique are
possessions that we want, to show ourselves off to advantage. Erik
Erikson describes adolescent love as "an attempt to arrive at a
definition of one's identity by projecting one's diffused ego images

on one another."[3] You learn about yourself by seeing yourself in the other person. How many of us are much past adolescent love when we decide to have children?

I certainly admit that part of my husband's attractiveness was that he found me desirable. I wanted to be loved and to be found lovable. Even if dragons are obsolete, I wanted someone to say that he would overcome all obstacles to be near me. Surely I must be special if someone is willing to support me for life. In marriage I hoped to find permanent affirmation of my own worth. What I am saying makes me sound like a good candidate for marriage counseling. Can anyone this self-centered and immature make a success of her marriage and rear children?

That certainly is a good question, but I maintain that there is absolutely nothing unusual about these self-centered feelings. Who does not demand self-gratification in marriage and in all relationships for that matter? That is why having a baby is such a turning point. With little previous practice in disinterestedly wanting the happiness of another, we assume a new life style in which we are defined as selflessly desiring to make our children happy—and that takes some getting used to. Babies come with so many needs that they force you to be "on call" almost all the time. Even if you will not actually "do" for the baby constantly, you still feel dutybound twenty-fours a day at the beginning. And that is an obligation any self-centered person in her right mind would fight.

It would be wonderful if we could all approach parenthood without mood swings and confused feelings, but most of us in our twenties and thirties are just getting used to being called Mrs. or "Ma'am." You spend so many of your early years waiting to be grown up that it is hard to realize when you have reached that point, unless trumpets blare it out. After a couple of decades of barely managing to dress yourself in time to go out, you find yourself in the position of having to dress someone else from scratch, in the same amount of time. Just when you are enjoying being a young woman because you can now drink and vote and drive a car, you find yourself not really young because another generation is climbing up behind you.

Let's go back briefly to the original question "Why have a baby?" It's clear by now that I think women have babies for all sorts of reasons having absolutely nothing to do with wanting to help a little person grow and develop into a happy, loving, productive adult. Some are seduced into motherhood by the promise of being special, of being fulfilled, of being loved; some have babies because that is what women are supposed to do. They usually do not become mothers because they want to care for someone else without any concern for personal benefit. If you have internalized the "fear of being left empty, and, more simply, that of being left,"[4] it is no wonder that a woman wants to have a baby to reaffirm herself. But by now the basic dilemma of motherhood is obvious: there usually is a big discrepancy between what the mother wants from the child and what the child needs from the mother. Of course mixed feelings accompany this whole process; they're inevitable.

No mother can avoid being absorbed in herself, nor would she want to, even if it were possible, because understanding oneself is essential to learning how to understand others. It is the tension between wanting self-gratification and learning to meet the needs of someone else that is important. This tension can be creative, for it can be the driving force behind all growth and development in the mother. Most movement in life is produced by being pulled first in one direction and then another, and what usually emerges is some constructive synthesis in which a marriage is effected between the real and the ideal. Mothering is a process whereby the woman is always pulled between some ideal notion of what the "good mother" should be and her own raw emotions. A gap always exists between the motives you can talk about and those that really torment you. And how you react to the baby is almost always tied up with what you expected from the baby.

Every expectation about what the baby will do for you and mean to you is bound to be frustrated at some time in some fashion. When this happens, one is generally inclined to curse the gods or take it out on the baby. But the more aware you are of what your expectations are, the better you can handle these frustrations. For example, if part of you wanted to have a baby to avoid loneliness you may be acutely disappointed when you fully realize how much being at home with a baby removes you from adult contact. Comprehending the difference between what you wanted from the baby and what you have received is essential if you are going to avoid being angry with her or him right from the beginning. I can remember expecting my newborn infant to snuggle into me, gratefully falling asleep after receiving my soothing caresses. I felt a good deal better when someone pointed out to me that infants just do not snuggle; they would have to be pretty well put together physically to have the motor ability necessary to burrow into a mother's arms. Babies are twitchy characters and automatically unable to meet such an expectation for several months. If you conceived a child because you wanted to hold on to your own youth, you may resent the fact that picking up the baby's toys and keeping her/him away from the steps consumes so much of your energy that you feel as if you have aged twenty years in a few months.

Now you may understand why you got so furious at the baby who was meant to smooth over troubles between you and your parents when he broke Grandma's favorite china figurine. Now you may understand why you boil inside when your "child of nature" says she wants to leave the beach after half an hour because "it's too hot." Doesn't she know that little children are supposed to like mud and kites and splashing? Instead of hurling epithets at your husband's car as he drives away to work, you may begin to understand more fully why you were so hurt when the husband who was supposed to honor you for life for giving him a beautiful child acted as if the baby's whining was entirely your fault. Remember, the child is incapable of providing the promised happy self-fulfillment because he "is in possession of no values, he can bestow none, with him the woman remains alone."[5] It does no good to blame him "for the deception of which she has been the victim and which he innocently exposes."[6]

It is tempting to want to blame someone when you do not feel the happy contented glow that is the supposed birthright of mothers. I remember the petulance I felt when I saw both of my daughters for the first time. Where was the intense closeness and affection mothers are supposed to feel toward their little ones? Somehow, I kept thinking I would love them if only they looked more human, and I held them responsible for not looking better when we met for the first time. I did not feel anything like the warm bond I was supposed to feel for this bundle newly removed from my body. As far as I was concerned, any relationship between that squirmy creature and my own bulging flesh was purely coincidental. I had intense feelings about my own protruding stomach, but something akin to indifference to this child. Over and over in my mind, I kept thinking that getting close to your baby was like getting close to your mother-in-law: everyone expects you to feel affection for a complete stranger. That expectation burdens the relationship from the very beginning, though I admit that babies have more going for them than a mother-in-law does.

Let me underline how much the average woman wants a baby so she can feel special, even though it is not an expectation that can be gratified. You may try to get over the disappointment by casting yourself as "Ms. Efficiency." You may try to order feedings, organize laundry, and even schedule free moments with a rigor that would confound the military, but what you are really trying to do is cope with your emotions—to order them. The routine is usually a secondary concern. I am not underestimating the physical demands that are part of this stage, but the emotional letdown after an event billed for so many months as the ultimate fulfillment can be *tremendous*. Physicians talk about postpartum depression as though it were a rare phenomenon; I think it is almost inevitable, but it can hit you anytime—two days after the baby is born or three years later.

As I see it, the most important job the new mother has is getting used to the emotional confusion that surrounds having a baby. You do this by learning how to live with ambivalence, by coming to expect that you will regularly have mixed feelings about yourself and your children. There is even such a thing as enjoying ambivalence. After all, many of one's expectations about the joys of having children do come true, even if they do not leave you feeling happy all the time. In very real ways, nursing a child can make you feel sensual, playing catch in the park can make you feel young, grandparents' pleasure can make you feel special, your husband's delight can make you feel loved and beautiful. It is, however, important to realize that these things are *equally* capable of causing you to feel the opposite. Children can enrich your opportunities for happy moments, but they cannot actually give you what you are not capable of giving yourself. A sense of purpose and fulfillment are never *given;* they develop in the individual gradually. And, most of all, living with your own ambivalence is a good preparation for dealing with the mixed feelings that your child is bound to have toward you in the future.

She wondered what was wrong with her, and why she should mind so much that she might, just once, have behaved unjustly with the children. What did it matter? . . . She sat defeating the enemy, restlessness. Emptiness. She ought to be thinking about her life, about herself. But she did not. Or perhaps she could not. . . . Resentment. It was poisoning her. (She looked at this emotion and thought it was absurd. Yet she felt it.) She was a prisoner.

—*Doris Lessing*[1]

3
The Anger-Depression-Guilt-Go-Round

"I love you." (Caress.) "I am furious with you." (Spanking. Tears.) "I'm sorry." Sounds like the script of a B movie, but this is no paperback pulp; this is the language and movement of real life. There are days when all of us, and especially parents, go around in emotional circles, riding the anger-depression-guilt-go-round. One moment you admire your child's prowess on the monkey bars; then you get furious (and I mean furious) because she yelled and stomped her feet and demanded ten cookies for a midmorning snack. She cries and flails her arms like an angry windmill. You respond with a mean wallop to her behind, then join in the crying because the day that looked so sunny and promising has been ruined. The edges of your mouth push downward in gloomy heaviness as the minutes tick by. For lunch, you decide to join that brooding five-year-old presence in having a peanut butter and jelly sandwich and ice cream loaded with chocolate sprinkles. You're miserable because you find it impossible to follow Dr.

Joyce Brothers' advice: "The best way to handle a temper tantrum is be sure you remain calm. If you can stay unemotional and go on doing what you have been doing calmly, as if nothing is happening, you will find that the tantrum is over much sooner and is less likely to recur as often."[2] You've muffed your latest diet with a vengeance. You hate yourself for not having the energy to fix a noncholesterol salad for lunch, one that would give your coronary plumbing a few extra years of pleasure.

Don't you love yourself? Don't you love your child? What kind of a model are you if you get angry just because your five-year-old made a childish demand? How dare she bring out your worst features. Lightning will strike you down because you are a thoroughly rotten mother. Did that spanking convince her brain and buttocks that women are sorry creatures, unworthy of imitation? Will she be a sadist, full of ire, because her mother was an avenging angel? How can you teach impulse control if you can't control your own impulses? Maybe you are the kind of woman who will bash in your kids' brains some fine April morning in the interval between "Captain Kangaroo" and "Sesame Street." Maybe you should just run away from this leering refrigerator, this house reeking of domesticity, a husband who expects you to act grown up, and children who look at you the way maggots size up a side of beef. You consider the virtues of reading a book titled *Parent Effectiveness Training: The "No-Lose" Program for Raising Responsible Children* and decide to scream instead.

Scream. I regularly feel like screaming out to protest all those "oughts" that choke me with guilt and that Janus-like god, anger-depression, who makes me feel like an emotional volcano. First, I get mad at myself, then I spill over, and the boiling inside scorches everyone around me. How galling it is to think of those social scientists sitting quietly behind their desks telling me to keep calm, not let the noisy confusion get to me. Those pontifical sentences like "If you're not a good person, chances are you may not be a very good parent"[3] make me wonder if I'm not the newest incarnation of the evil mother. In my more sane moments, however, I have come to realize that my feelings are normal. They must be normal, or else we have a nation of crazy mothers. No, I think my feelings belong in the category of "normal crazy."

"Normal crazy" describes those emotions and thoughts that deviate from what the literature and popular opinion hold up as ideal or good behavior. Yet I know everyone else feels them, too, for I have spent countless hours collecting anecdotes and prevalence statistics over coffee and in cocktail-party laboratories. It may sound peculiar to speak of "normal crazy" behaviors, but I am very serious about the term. Much of our behavior deserves this label.

In this chapter, and the next three, I shall be talking about the "normal crazy" behavior of parents. We must stop being ashamed of our real emotions; we must start getting out into the open some of the worries child-rearing books completely ignore. M. Esther Harding says that "our textbooks of psychology are concerned chiefly with the complexes and conflicts in the child and deal with these to the almost complete exclusion of the mother's side of the problem."[4] Right on. This silence is related, of course, to the role problems mentioned in the first chapter. Since women are supposed to be fulfilled by motherhood and in charge of the family's happiness, it seems to be entirely their fault if they feel inadequate or the children don't act right.

Even those books with a section at the beginning titled "Parents Have Feelings, Too" always manage to convey the impression that any negative feelings in a parent should last only as long as it takes to read the five-page chapter. Apparently, mothers can become cross but not ferociously angry, glum but not morose, grouchy and irritable but never truculent and caustic. It is almost as if the authors were worried that if they referred to a particular emotion by the strongest possible adjective, they might unleash hideous maternal furies and provide a license for violence. But recognizing the intensity of an emotion does not mean that it will be acted out in a nonconstructive way; in fact, emotional self-awareness is the first step toward impulse control. There is little difference between my wrath and that of the mother of a battered child, but the difference in how we handle our rage is tremendous. All emotions cannot be handled constructively all the time, but working in that direction should be a goal for the mother. And identifying the feelings and thoughts that certain experiences produce is the first step in figuring out what to do with them.

Back to anger, depression, and guilt. I chose to talk about this nasty little trio, not just because of my interest in mystical numbers, but because I have become convinced that these feelings play such an important part in all mother-child relationships. Most adults reach physical maturity with an awful lot of angry feelings stored up in them. How many of us really got rid of the anger and rebellious impulses of adolescence by the time we hit our twenties and thirties? We may have become "socialized," but there are legions of horned, red creatures bobbing around in our ids, waiting for some event to set them loose. We have learned to sublimate (rechannel the energy of) many of these feelings by hitting a ball with a racket, turning a rock record on full blast, or tailgating in the supermarket parking lot. But it is important not to forget either our capacity for a temper tantrum or the pleasure that cursing, hitting, yelling, and scratching can produce. Just because married adults have removed themselves geographically from their parents' hearth and the scene of past temper tantrums, just because you have begun to learn how to live with your own angry aggressive impulses and those of your spouse without having a full-scale fight each day, and just because you feel happy and loved when the sun is shining—these facts do not mean that you have mellowed into a tolerant woman, full of *natural* maternal affection.

Anger and depression are Siamese twins. Your style may be to hurl your feelings in the direction of someone (or something) else, or you may keep them inside and punish yourself for the torment you feel. Depression will never go away as long as there is anger. Most of us alternate between feeling angry and feeling depressed about the things that bother us. There is a tendency to get angry at little things we can name and get depressed over big troubles, because they are overwhelming. Betty Friedan's discussion of the "terrible tiredness" that sent so many housewives to doctors in her chapter "The Problem That Has No Name" suggests that mothers might have a tendency to choose depression over out-and-out anger as a way of handling their feelings, because their frustrations are vague requests for self-fulfillment and non-specific responses to the role of being a woman.[5] Depression and anger will not go away just because our social mythology describes functioning adults as even-tempered, nonmoody people. And guilt builds up when we fail to live up to society's and our own expectations. Guilt is something we feel when we think we have failed or been inadequate in an area of importance. But there just is no magic age—not twenty-one or thirty-five or seventy-eight—when emotional equilibrium is ours without having to work for it.

There are many specific reasons for a mother to get angry or depressed. If she grew up indoctrinated with the notion that "mother is the leader and *expert* in child rearing and has a primary concern with *intrafamilial harmony* and *reduction of family tensions*"[6] (emphases mine), it is not surprising that a woman might easily become angry and distraught in the face of her responsibilities. She alone in the family is burdened with the responsibility for everyone's bliss. But no one can handle a job impossible in its very description, and most women feel anything but "expert." "Society can't expect the impossible," she may guiltily conclude. "*Someone* must be coping with family tensions and unhappiness. It must be me. Everyone else seems to know what they're doing." What follows? Tears, fatigue, hair pulling, and a trip to the doctor for a "nervous stomach," where she gets diagnosed as being a "crock" because he can't find anything *physically* wrong with her. Or if she can't take comfort in realizing she, too, is in the process of growing and developing, she may give up and become the family character—"Mom," an emotional wheeler and dealer, who avoids demands by being demanding. It is so easy to go from being on the defensive to being offensive that many mothers are scared of themselves, for themselves, of their children, and for their children.

There is so much if/then thinking in our lives that we are accustomed to believe that if only we were happy *then* we would be loving; if only we were this, *then* we would be that. I don't know whether it is our Puritan inheritance, or what, but we always seem to need to talk about good or bad, right or wrong, with no middle ground, and we busily spell out the circumstances and conditions necessary for fulfillment or ruin. If I am unloved, then I must be evil. If I am loved, then I must be good. If I am angry, then I am a rotten mother. If I am depressed, then I am an unsuccessful wife. If I feel guilty, then I have done something bad.

Take the old slogan "children equal fulfillment" seriously, and you will be totally unprepared for the fact that anger, depression, guilt, and a host of other "improper" feelings still live in you. Children are never prizes proving your own excellence, value, goodness, or emotional stability. Stop thinking in these terms. Start understanding yourself better, and try to experiment with acting differently in ways that occur to you as a result of these new insights. When you are angry, depressed, and/or guilty, *there are good reasons why.* Find out what they are. If you can figure out what impossible behavioral expectations have been drummed into your head, you can do something constructive with those seemingly "wrong" feelings.

What causes reactions in your spleen? Maybe setting down my own experiences will make you aware of some of the "normal crazy" thoughts that have bothered you:

> *Until I had my first child, I never realized how much crying, wailing, whining, and screaming can get on one's nerves. I become a purple monster when I hear those vile noises, and I want to cover the baby's face with a pillow to silence her. Listening to my child's rage reminds me of my own. I want to spank, shake, scratch, and hit her head against the radiator. Her demands for help and comfort have made me more demanding; I yearn for the pleasure of sniveling, yelping, growling, and blubbering. Oh, how many times have I been convinced*

that her shrieks were malicious, deliberate attempts to show up my inadequacies, to lay bare my raw jumping nerves.

I resent the fact that all other women seem to get what I crave and never seem to grasp. When they are pregnant, they always look more beautiful and fragile than I do. When they cradle their infants in their arms, they seem to know what they're doing. When someone says, "How sweet your baby is," they never seem ready to punch that person in the face and say, "I hate the baby, and I hate you for thinking that that drooling, oozing, frantic mess of cells is sweet." Yet I regularly play out the ritual and say, "How sweet," when I am seething inside. It is as if I were in a never-ending competition. I push myself and my children toward a finishing line that we can never reach. We are locked into an eternal struggle which demands that I smile at the right time, that my daughters say "please" and "thank you" at all the appropriate moments, that I offer my baby strained meat and vegetables, even though she hates the taste and I dislike the smell. I struggle to be soft, and feel more and more like a bland marshmallow. Am I destined to live out my days forever judging and being judged? I see someone else's child, and when she is happy with his gurgling sounds, I pray that that child will be mean so I can sit back and enjoy the misery and anguish of his mother. Instead of pastel thoughts and feelings, my psyche is ablaze with murderous color.

The embryo grew into a toddler when I was not looking. She is no longer content with my presence, but wants to "bring my friend over for a drink." Just when I was getting used to my child, I was forced to abide the presence of other children, "her friends." They knock at the door and demand a snack: "We want some juice, cookies, and a popsicle, like we had yesterday." I feel like throwing it in their faces. Greedy parasites, all of them. The six-year-old across the street comes over to play with my child; she allots ten seconds to each toy *and leaves after fifteen minutes, saying that "you don't have many interesting toys." My child is in hysterics because "my friend left and won't come back and play with me." And I feel like killing because a child has made me feel so inadequate.*

After considerable hemming and hawing, I decided to go back to work part-time. A friend mentions how much she envies me my outside contacts but finishes her comments with "I want to take care of my children myself until they get to first grade. When they get screwed up, I'll know that I did it myself." My insides bleed. Is she hinting that I am deficient in the maternal instinct department? How scary to think that if anything goes wrong (and something surely will) you are solely responsible. It's overwhelming enough to convince anyone to work full-time and overtime so one can blame the babysitter for all character deficiencies. Am I that powerful? Must I live out my days forever blaming and being blamed? I want to run away—from the children, from these peeling walls, from myself. In days gone by, we carried our ancestors' ashes around with us. Now my hands are free, but my superego (or conscience, or whatever name you want to give to that man who rules my innards by making marks in his ledger) is burdened by so many hopes, failings, expectations, and "oughts."

My daughter spits a mixture of strained plums and sweet potatoes in my face. Maybe she is trying to tell me how she feels about me. She laughs, and I resent being the butt of her joke. Why doesn't she like food that is supposed to be good for her? Doesn't she know that new tastes are like new adventures? I feel like reading her some of the child-rearing literature so that she will start acting as she's supposed to.

I am not sure whether I believe in God. I do not want to give Him up, but I have so many questions about the religious beliefs I was taught as a child. If only I did not have a child, I could relegate my doubts, misgivings, and skepticism to the back recesses of my mind, and hope that time would hold the answers that analysis and argument do not. But I cannot put off thinking about these things and let my life slide by, because I have to decide whether my child is going to go to Sunday school and say prayers before going to bed. I hate God for making life so hard for me. I'll bet God is a child!

Santa Claus, I hate you. Why should you get the credit for my hard work? It is important for my children to think that someone besides fickle Mommy and Daddy wants to watch over them and give them things, but why should good fairies bring out their dimples instead of me?

We mothers have received a very bad press. All those nasty stepmothers in the fairy tales are just literary devices for bringing out the hate and anger that children have for their own mothers. Perhaps I am the personification of nastiness because I feel like doling out poisoned apples, putting my children to sleep with a prick of a black-magic needle, and locking my daughters up in a tower.

Soon after my favorite grandmother died, my own mother became critically ill. Maybe I will be next in line? It's not fair that those two buffer generations are leaving me feeling so vulnerable. I loathe my children's smooth cheeks and vitality. Cammie is scared of death, but how can I comfort when I need comforting?

I always hated being kidded when I was a child, and yet I find myself doing the same things. I think things like "I'm not going to come back" or "Maybe I'll stop loving you" and then take them back before they are said. Or I'll play at being a Mommy dragon and act more frightening than I intend to. I want to be loving, but I want to eat my child up. I want to be sensitive to her needs, but I laugh at her mistakes and bring on her tears, which I cannot tolerate. Can't she take a joke? Who am I kidding? Why am I kidding? A phony laughter regularly blankets the serious, earnest, morbid self that I cannot tolerate.

I offer my children, my goddesses, gifts to appease them and the fates. What am I trying to buy from them? Gifts do not equal love, but they are symbols that I play around with. I make impossible demands: "If you are good, then Mommy will buy you a Snoopy sweat shirt. If you are good, then . . ." "If I give you gifts, then you will love me. If I am good, then . . ." But they want more, and I want more. Maybe they do not love me because they do not always try to be good.

I sit in front of the television and hungrily wish that Mr. Rogers would sing to me "It's you I like; it's every part of you; your skin, your eyes, your feelings, that are old or new." Can I seduce my children's father figure? With jealous indignation, I want to shout out that the words of another song are too simple and too complicated: "I'm taking care of you, taking good care of you. For once, I was very little, too. Now I take care of you." Take care of me, Mr. Rogers, please.

"If you love your baby and want to be close to her, of course you will breast-feed"—that advice sticks in my craw. I try so hard to be loving; I stick my tumescent flesh into the baby's hole, but I resent the demands that "demand feeding" forces me to endure. I am forever dressing and undressing. Am I satisfying? I am too proud to ask for help, but I wonder if my equipment is adequate to the job. Surreptitiously, I sneak a peak at those busty bulges in other nursing mothers; I have a locker room mentality. I offer succor, but the baby seems unwilling to work for it and seems to prefer bottled satisfaction to my skittish suckle.

Every day, I want to whack my children over the head with words: "After all I have done for you" or "I am doing this for your own good" or "Mother knows what's best." What orgastic pleasure in a good put-down!

"Who do you like best," I'd like to ask my daughter. *"Mommy or Daddy?"* She squirms, and I ask for confirmation; I set up competition. My heart and eyes and gestures ask the question, even when I don't open my mouth.

My daughter is proud of her bowel movements; they look like pliant brown snakes. She once played with her feces; I wonder how it feels to be so oblivious to social convention. I'm revolted by the memory, so I push her toward toilet training. I push her toward the restraint that I find difficult. I want to be vulgar and dirty and obnoxious, but I don't want to because I am proper.

Bottles are convenient. Why am I so worried that everyone will think that she is too big to walk around with one? Am I too indulgent or just too inefficient to wean my little girl at the proper time? A bottle comforts her when she is ready for sleep. They're spillproof, though cups are not. Why am I so concerned about what people think of me? Should I let her take her pleasure where she can, or should I make her socially acceptable?

I can't stand it when my children are sick. I feel responsible for every germ or virus that sneaks into my home. How dare they conspire to make me look bad! Did I give my children bad genes—weak muscles, infected tonsils, flat feet, sensitive ears, allergies? I beg their mercy for my failings. Why do I always have to feel like a failure?

I want my children to be generous but not to give away any of their toys. They should be loving but stop short of loving anyone more than they care for me. They should be independent but never do anything without telling me about it first. I want to be generous, but why should they have new dresses when I need one, too? I try to be loving, yet sometimes I deny them embraces out of personal pique. How can I have a life of my own and still be attached to them? Contradictions stalk me on all sides.

The neighborhood children are sprawled all over the stoop. They're busily telling "knock-knock" jokes. They giggle and fall to the ground, amazed at the nonsense rhyme my daughter has concocted. I feel left out. I wish I had that many friends. I want some fun. I pick up the discarded popsicle sticks and feel like a drudge. When the chuckles have gone away, I lecture them about being too loud.

I want my children to like the baby-sitter so I don't have to feel guilty when I leave them to go to work. The older one came home beaming with pleasure after spending the morning making cranberry bread. "I even cracked the eggs," said my daughter, obviously rubbing in the fact that I have never let her do that. I'm jealous of my sitter for baking my daughter's "Gold Medal memories." I'm jealous, yet pleased.

The magazines say, "Relax and enjoy your children," but I sit there with a scorecard. How popular are my daughters? Is one too stuck-up? Is the other one too awkward when she is running? I wonder how they'll do on I.Q. tests. Are they happy most of the time? Maybe the two-year-old is always going to have a rococo figure. Is it too late to start swimming lessons or too early? Will they always whine then they are not getting their own way? I tell myself daily to relax and enjoy my children.

I keep telling my daughters that mothers and fathers need privacy—"Go out and play. Mommy wants to be by herself for a few minutes." Now my five-year-old says, "I am going up to my room for a few minutes because I feel like being private." What does she do when she is alone? What is she thinking about? I feel left behind.

I can close my eyes and still hear my father yelling at the toddler me, because I spilled milk all over the Sunday dinner table. How I resented his self-righteousness, yet I echo the same tone when my daughters spill juice on the floor. I find their clumsiness intolerable. I sound like Ms. Prune Face when

I shout, "You mean you dropped the glass again?" but I can't stop the angry words from spewing out.

Am I paranoid? I keep thinking that the dentist is watching me to see that my children get six-month checkups, that the pediatrician assesses my children's ears and throats to see if I am doing a good job. Detergent and bleach companies urge me to get those play clothes "really clean." Don't they realize that I don't mind a little grey? Am I buying the right vitamins for my children? I want to strangle dancing cereal boxes that make me worry about breakfast variety. Everyone is after me. I want to hide, but the Good Humor bells follow me everywhere.

Jealousy, rage, envy, anger, depression, confusion, competition, guilt, sadism, and narcissism may not be as "normal" as apple pie, but they are normally present in all mothers. It's not whether you have these emotions; it's "just" how you handle them that matters. We all have secret thoughts and feelings that intrude on our interactions with our children. Just about all mothers feel inadequate and try to compensate by posing as superwomen, feel competitive and offset this emotion by being extrapassive, feel resentful, then find themselves being oversolicitous in a syrupy kind of way. We blame and feel blamed; we judge and feel judged.

So-called negative emotions are like physical pain; they let you know what is going on inside of you. You will never be able to stop having negative feelings, but you can start appreciating their diagnostic value; they are trying to tell you something about yourself. If you were disappointed that breast-feeding wasn't the lusty experience you had wanted, think about why you were encouraged to have that expectation instead of being annoyed that your baby was less than enthusiastic about you and your milk. When you find it difficult to "relax and enjoy your children," don't blame them for making you feel tense. Ask yourself, "Why am I trying so hard? Who do I want to please?" If you find yourself wanting to buy your child's love with a present, don't be so angry when it's not appreciated, but think about why you are worried about being lovable.

Suppose you get angry at your child for being overly "proper" with her/his peers and then feel depressed and guilty because you seem incapable of rearing a "spontaneous" child. No use feeling generally rotten. Maybe what you need to do is examine your hopes. Are you expecting the child to act one way at home, one way with other children, one way with one set of grandparents, a different way with the other set of grandparents, and still a fifth way when your high school cronies come to visit? Once you have tried a little introspection, you might have a better idea of what the problem is, and you might even stop expecting perfection in yourself and your child. Learning how to adapt your behavior to different people and different situations takes time and practice. You and your child both might profit from a few shared words about how hard it is to know what will please different people and what will please you.

If you have jealous, mean, and paranoid moments, there may be some temptation to wonder whether you are any more grown up than your children are. But parents are far from being as helpless as babies, even if they often feel inadequate. Parents already know much about emotions and what it's like to grow up. If an infant shrieks out her/his rage and the mother responds with rage of her own, she is still more mature than the baby because she can put a value on her response, think about causes, about more appropriate behavior, and decide to act differently the next time the baby cries. In fact, it is the mother's scrutiny of her own conduct and her attempts to experiment with handling her reactions that influence the child's development over the long run. This is the single most important aspect of all growth and development in a family. *While parents consciously try to help their children grow and develop, they cannot help dealing with their own conflicts and inadequacies, and achieve a new level of maturity in this very process.*

A child's emotions, which are raw, spontaneous, and relatively free of social artifice, often reawaken past feelings and conflicts in the parent. Norman Paul says that the parent will "oscillate between experiencing the child's feelings as his own and drawing back into an objective view of the feelings."[7] This dance between the real and the ideal, between the present and the remembered, is the key to growing up as a parent. The mother has a second chance to resolve some of the insecurities that remain from her own uneven childhood experiences. Therese Benedek, concerned with the psychology of parenthood, talks about the parent's development occurring through the repetition of childhood conflict: ". . . the reworking of the childhood conflicts leads to resolving them."[8] How true. I doubt whether you ever really resolve anything completely, but watching the satisfaction that your child gets from sucking and being cuddled will tell you something about your own nurturing needs. Her struggles for independence will strike a responsive chord if you are still trying to find yourself. Her curiosity about genital differences may reactivate your own feelings of shame and guilt.[9] We are constantly rethinking, analyzing, and re-evaluating our past in terms of our personal, present needs and those of our children, with a view to reciprocal growth and development. (Since I am focusing on mother-child relationships, I do not mention fathers very much, which makes what I say artificial, for any talk of the mutual influence of developing parents on developing children presupposes a simultaneous growth in the spouses' relationship to each other.)

When I talk about analyzing and re-evaluating oneself, it may sound more complicated than it is. Ninety-nine per cent of all mothers already know that *children change us* and force us to grow up. We all try to figure out how to do things better so the child will have a better example to follow, and we live in the eternal hope that our children will grow up with fewer weaknesses than we have. It is the very process of trying to accomplish this that moves us all toward increased maturity.

A good example is how we handle our own anger.* The first time my child threw a temper tantrum and I responded with one of my own, I panicked. I remember thinking, "How can I teach her how to act right if I can't control myself?" I was depressed for days. Could I become an even-tempered woman after twenty-odd years of bitchiness? I began to think a good deal about angry behavior. Flexing your temper is probably as normal as flexing your muscles; it proves that your emotional system is working (not however that you want to exercise it every day). In fact, being able to express anger is quite important psychologically to us all. You can never completely get rid of anger, but you can get rid of some angry feelings before they build up and an eruption occurs that produces additional unpleasantness.

I like to scream, so I began to encourage my daughter to scream every now and then, just for fun, and to sing at the top of her lungs. I like to curse too, so I decided that we should both use angry words to get rid of feelings. Since "damn," "crap," "shit," and other favorites are frowned on by our society, I encouraged her to make up her own. I told her it did not make any difference what words were used as long as they showed how angry you were. Now I often hear "You are nothing but a chocolate-covered, yucky meatball" being angrily hurled at me by my daughter. I respond by saying that she is "a rotten, stinking, tuna fish sandwich." Such angry, creative exchanges usually lead to giggles and great relief of mutual tension.

Sometimes I use stories to illustrate for my daughter what makes mothers angry and little girls furious. My daughter enjoys stories about little girls her own age—how they feel, what they do, how their mommies and daddies and siblings feel, and so on. Change the name, and you can weave into story form all the events, both physical and psychological, of your child's day. It works out quite

---

* Anger is an especially big problem for women because they are prohibited from sounding angry. It is unfeminine behavior—"People don't like fussy little girls. Who will ever want to marry a sourpuss like you?" As a result, women tend to be overwhelmed by their own feelings and avoid thinking about them. It is "easier" in this society for a woman to be long-suffering than to be angry.

well if you ask your child, "How do you think the little girl felt when her mommy did that?" She and I sometimes pretend to be monsters and tell each other all the angry, horrible, bad things we did that day to the daddies, mommies, and children in the neighborhood. I find that these pretend games are a good device for helping the child understand how she feels inside. It also teaches her that the world won't fall apart if she lets some of those powerful emotions surface while we are "making believe."

This is not a how-to-do-it book, so I am not going to try to explain all the ways you can deal with anger, yours or your child's. Hitting balls, painting "mad" pictures, and wrestling sometimes work for us; different things work at different times. It is not so much what you try but *that* you try. You cannot wish negative feelings away, but you can deliberately work with them on a conscious level and experiment with new ways of relieving them. Ironically, when you stop expecting to be the "perfect" or "good" mother, you really do have more of a chance to develop your own personality and your child's. I had tremendous expectations of what kind of mother I would be, and was angry, depressed, and filled with guilt—usually simultaneously—when I felt myself failing. Once I could appreciate how grown up I had actually become, because I could keep my screams at a lower pitch and indulge in them less often, I found myself acting like a coping mother. It was then that I also came to realize that something else was getting in the way of my functioning. I not only expected the impossible of myself, but part of me always demanded perfection in my children because they were really "me." I expected to behave correctly—to be the "good" mother—and my children were supposed to be "good," too, or otherwise I would look "bad." My children weren't supposed to be depressed or angry; they weren't supposed to have violent swings of mood. I began finally to wonder why I always expected them to be better than I had been as a child. And this proved a profitable investigation for both me and my children.

Each parent has to deal in his own way with the
positive as well as the negative revelations of himself in the child.

4

The Better Part of Me

I remember thumbing through one of those simple, cheerful
pamphlets that decorate most pediatricians' offices and reading,
"The baby is a kind of extension of yourself on which you focus
hopes and energies."[2] How true, and yet how anemic those words
sounded when I thought about my own experience. Sometimes I
wonder if fiction isn't more real than the idealized, sterilized,
sentimentalized accounts of parent-child exchanges that fill drug-
store news racks and the professional journals. This single sentence
casually thrown into a section on "learning to be a parent doesn't
take unusual skills" and "no one really expects your home to be in
apple-pie order *all* the time" (emphasis mine) does nothing to
prepare you for the very real, complicated emotions that the
mother in *Up the Sandbox* describes so beautifully:

And with each feeding, each soothing, each moment we live together,
I grow into him. My spirit oozes out, I feel myself contracting and
him expanding, and the ties between us solidify. And I am almost his
possession. . . . My selfish purposes are also served, instead of being,
as I was before I conceived a child, a bit of dark matter orbiting aim-

lessly, brooding on my own molecular disintegration, I am now a proper part of ordinary society.[3]

"Real" emotions may be more alarming than those alluded to in supermarket magazines, but they are also the stuff of which poetry is made. One has some sense of the rhythms of life in this passage—the desire to be absorbed by the child's promise of perfection, the flesh's search for immortality, the symbiotic bonds that connect but also shackle, the hope that the child will give the mother's life a sense of purpose, the parent's struggle to be selfless rather than selfish.

These sentences scream out the identity dilemma of being a parent. The child seems the answer to one's "own molecular disintegration," but it is also responsible for the parent's spirit oozing out and contracting. The mother grows into the child, yet it is the parent's success or failure, rather than the child's, that is the focus of attention. The child is both the mother's toy and the tyrant controlling her life. The mother can lose her identity to her child or absorb the child's vitality for her self-aggrandizement. It is no wonder that women feel ambivalence in the role of mother, since parent-child relationships are so full of conflicting pulls. All our thoughts, feelings, and actions continually bob from one point to another as we understand ourselves better and try to effect some kind of balance between self-realization and helping the child "realize" herself/himself. Seeing the child as an extension of oneself is a developmental stage each parent must get through before she can permit the child to have a separate identity.

My child is me, and I am my child. As I have come to understand what this really means to me, I find that I am more and more able to handle the "normal crazy" behavior implicit in this kind of conceptualization. Psychiatrists talk about the newborn's inability to tell where she or he ends and where the mother begins (autistic thinking); the breast is part of her or him. The infant sees everything in relationship to herself/himself. My daughter's chin, which juts out like my own, is my chin. When friends comment that she is pretty and mention at another time that she looks like me, I am ecstatic. If she has beauty, I am comely. If she is graceful, I must be graceful. Her good humor is proof of my own. Her shyness is my own revisited. How many of us are ever devoid of autistic thinking? We continue to see the world in relation to ourselves, even when we are old enough to distinguish the parts from the whole, to separate the essentials from the particulars, to know the difference between our reactions and the stimuli that provoked them. Our children are parts of us, and we constantly project our expectations onto them.

Surely the child could not be so energetic, curious, whimsical, and athletic, if there were not a piece of these talents in the parent. Each obvious chromosomal link between us and our children strengthens the feeling of kinship that we have with them. You may detest the baby's crying, but you begin to admire his spirit because it reminds you of your own. Your daughter's reluctance to eat certain foods may annoy you, but you may try to convince yourself that it is because she is endowed with an exquisitely refined palate. You look toward the child to confirm your virtues—real and imagined—and in seeing yourself in miniature, you hope to find proof of your basic lovability. If the Christ Child can make us love God, maybe that diminutive self, a daughter or a son, will bring love to the full-grown self called a parent.

Since the baby is loaded down with the parent's expectations, there is usually a tremendous pressure to see the baby as exceptional, special, out-of-the-ordinary. Even a mother who once ridiculed her parents for always talking about growth charts and averages may find herself making comparisons between her child and someone else's. To be the mother of the tallest boy in the kindergarten class is such a pleasure. I remember the disappointment I felt when the pediatrician said that our two-year-old was in the fiftieth percentile on the growth charts as far as weight and height were concerned. Who wants to have *the* normal child? I resented the implication that my child could be average in any possible way. Certainly my children were destined to be above average. I remember being obsessed with those graphs pinpointing the average time that the child first sits, begins to crawl, and walks without holding on to the furniture (though I would have denied this obsession vehemently had anyone pointed it out). Toilet training was particularly painful, since our society places such a high premium on a world without smells. You keep hoping your child will be out of diapers before anyone else's, so you can gloat. I don't happen to mind soggy pants, but I was haunted by the need to order my child's bodily functions just the way the nurses did mine after I had the baby. I wanted her to be ahead of schedule (I'm not sure whose schedule, surely not nature's), just the way I wanted to have a bowel movement by the third postpartum day to please the nurses, and in some perverse way, prove my own worth.

Most of us are secretly worried that if the child is not special, then maybe we as parents are not. What results is a frantic and highly amusing attempt to see all the child's characteristics as special. If the child is little, you start talking about the joys of a "dainty" girl. If the baby is big, you pride yourself on having a "healthy" child. If the little heir is active, you describe him as "alert and intelligent." A quiet child becomes a "contented" child. If teeth come early, you note how precocious the baby is. If teeth come late, you start talking about how decay-free they will be when they get here. If the child is slow saying her or his first word, you start looking for proof that the baby is especially adroit physically. And, of course, if the child is slow in physical development, then you talk about how busy the baby is experimenting with different sounds and stringing different vocalizations together in sentence form. If your toddler has blue eyes, then blue eyes are beautiful. If your daughter has brown eyes then you may start referring to them as "darkly seductive." Most parents would put the best advertising men to shame with their public-relations skills.

It works both ways, of course, seeing yourself in your offspring. You can look at your mirror image and assign value to what you see, but all reflections are bound to expose other aspects of yourself that are bitterly bothersome and problematic. Benedek talks about the child at birth being an enigma. "He represents hope and promise for self-realization and at the same time he forewarns that he may expose not one's virtues but one's faults."⁴ The alter ego has all the emotions of the ego. The child has the potential for having the same kind of problems as the parent. And it can be quite a shock to see what annoys you in yourself acted out in front of you. What you might prefer to forget about past hurts or present failings stands there demanding attention. A father who hated spelling is forced to think about it again when his daughter asks him whether "e" comes before "i" or the other way round. The man who can't balance a budget starts lecturing his son about saving part of each week's allowance. A mother with insomnia has a daughter who has trouble going to sleep. I have never had much patience for puzzles, and my child cries with huge frustration after five minutes of fooling around with the pieces. Yet my reaction is sometimes one of indignation. How dare she have difficulty with a puzzle "for children four to eight years of age" once she is four years old! Doesn't she realize she will grow up just as unmechanical as I am, if she continues to act in this way?

I love ice cream and sweets. My two daughters share my enthusiasms. Somehow, they never seem to muster up the same eagerness for carrot sticks and celery hearts. If a mother feels "deprived" when she is told to omit desserts, it is awfully hard not to make the child feel "deprived" when similar limits are set. Not having dessert for supper then becomes the ultimate punishment. Suddenly, the next generation is saddled with the food habits and prejudices of the parents, and you may not even realize how it happened. Not only do you hate your own extra bulges, but your child's rounded figure reminds you, with every glance, of your own weakness. You worry that your child will feel the loneliness of growing up chubby, and badger the child with threats of an ugly future because you resent the fact that she or he lacks discipline. This all-too-familiar scenario in our snack-oriented society graphically demonstrates how a child can dramatize a parent's problem simply by imitating a parent's behavior. This time, however, instead of receiving compliments for personifying parental virtue, the child is battered by the rage a mother or father has felt about his/her own failings.

I expect my children to be like me, *only better*. I want them to be disciplined and steady in their work habits, even though I work in spurts. I tend to complain and indulge in tears when I am hurt, but I expect my children not to whine or tattle on their friends. I am prejudiced about all sorts of things, but I expect to raise daughters who are free of bias. I don't want my children to be tormented by the guilt feelings I have, yet I resent it when they don't seem sorry enough for some transgression of my will. I seduce my friends with cocktails and dinners, but I resent it when my child "buys" a friend's attentions with apple juice and animal crackers. All sorts of "normal crazy" expectations and fantasies follow from the notion that the child is an extension of the parent.

Often I've realized that things which are the most emotionally upsetting to me are usually connected with some unresolved business in my own growing up. We tend to want to supply our children with what we did not have. If your parents had a cluttered apartment, you may want to provide your child with an ordered, neat home that she/he can be proud of. If your mother did not pay much attention to you (or so you imagined), then as a mother you may become even a bit oversolicitous. If your father was anything but a "fun" parent, you may be inclined to be overindulgent and silly in your push for mandatory Sunday outings. In any event, it should come as no surprise that psychoanalytic investigations have revealed that parents expect their children to have trouble with the same things that worried them.[5]

Several months ago, I was bemoaning the lack of cordiality in my neighbors. Over coffee with the one neighbor I had gotten to know well, I was going on about everyone's indifference to everyone else. I had visions (not very original ones) of my whole family dead and rotting inside the house and no one even noticing the stench. I was feeling particularly sorry for myself. As I looked through the kitchen window, I saw the child of one of my indifferent neighbors tease my own child. It was like being thrashed with a horsewhip. Tears flooded my eyes. There must be a conspiracy to make me and my child miserable. I wanted to rush out and hit and scream. Yet my daughter was busily catching linden moths with her friend long before I regained my composure. I had managed to project my own feelings onto my daughter's experience. Her hurts were mine, and *magnified* by all sorts of remembered hurts. I interpreted the reserve of my New England neighbors as deliberate attempts to tease me. "Will I be popular?" was mixed up in my mind with "Will my daughter be popular?" Though this particular event may seem more crazy than normal, it helped me grow up as a mother. I forced myself to disentangle my present feelings about my neighbors from my adolescent (but still very much present) concerns about being popular (whatever that means). And I tried to separate (at least in my own mind) my worries from my daughter's life. She needed help in being able to handle teasing, and trying to help her gave me added insight into myself. We talked about what teasing means and why some people like to say things that upset you. I needed to realize, too, how inclined we are to take out on a child the feelings we have for that child's parents.

While it may seem abnormal to think, "I am my child, and my child is me," this tendency in all parents does have a very constructive use. Just as negative feelings can tell you something about unfinished business in your own development, your reactions to your child's weaknesses and virtues also have a diagnostic value. In a book titled, *Normal Children and Mothers,* Irving Harris mentions that both the mothers and the fathers in his study "invariably showed evidence of using their parenthood to continue or to resolve, through their children, some aspects of their own growing up, and therefore each of their several children might represent a somewhat different aspect of their past."[6] I find that having two children with very different personalities and looks has allowed me two different opportunities to look at my own strengths and frailties. In one child, I can examine the artistic, articulate, vulnerable part of me; in the other, I see the curious, exuberant, stubborn part of me. But I do have to keep fighting the tendency to "label" one child as verbal, moody, and physically slow, and the other as inarticulate, cheerful, and athletic. When you have more than one child, I think you are inclined to apportion various personality characteristics among the children so you can work out specific feelings with specific children. This can be dangerous because we all tend to act out the labels that we were stuck with in our early years. Thinking this way can deny the real possibility that an athletic child may be physically slow in the first year of life. It's possible for a moody child to be a cheerful child; it's possible, too, to be verbal one moment and quite inarticulate thirty seconds later.

Each child can help you grow up in a special way, but you do have to guard against sticking the tags on too quickly. It is especially dangerous when we label our sons as the ones who should act out our aggressive, ambitious feelings and our daughters as the ones who should represent the domestic, affectionate parts of us. If the mother starts thinking her son is the boy she might have been, she may weigh him down with her frustrated career goals, just as a father may burden his daughter with his own need to be a social success. Labeling minimizes both the parents' and the child's chances for working through the fact that seemingly contradictory traits can exist in the same person. Labeling limits the personality. For example, my father came to represent the "angry" person in his family. Very early on, everyone agreed he sounded just like his father, who was famous for his terrific temper (at least that was the family myth). I grew up wondering if my father had ever had the opportunity not to be angry. Perhaps his first cry for milk was described as "What lungs that boy has; he's just like his hot-tempered father!"

We project our thoughts and feelings on others because we tend to assume that everyone is like we are or like someone we know. It is easy for the mother to read into the baby's behavior all her own hopes, fears, and anxieties, just the way you do when you describe what you see in those inkblot tests. But as Simone de Beauvoir said:

What is in any case remarkable and distinguishes this relation of mother and baby from all other human relations is the fact that at first the baby itself takes no active part in it: its smiles, its babble, have no sense other than what the mother gives them; whether it seems charming and unique, or tiresome, commonplace, and hateful, depends upon her, not upon the baby.[7]

I do not completely agree with her here because I think that even unborn babies respond *actively* to the mother's movements and hormones; babies do react to the breast, bubbles in their stomachs, and churning in their bowels in unique ways. But she is right when she points out that it is the parent who labels the behavior and who assigns a *value* to the child's first attempts to respond to this benignly hostile environment.

If you feel basically good about your child, you read all sorts of nice things into her or his uncoordinated efforts to function outside the uterus. You say, "The baby is happy when fed," "yawns with contentment," "relaxes to music," "peers through those little red slits with intelligence," and so forth. But if you are feeling mean, and everyone does at one point or another, you might say, "The baby keeps dropping the rattle to annoy me," "he looks at me as if he already knows more than I do," "the way she ignored that present proves what an ungrateful child she really is," "he laughs as if he were making fun of me," and so forth.

Not only does the mother project her own reactions on the child, responding to the negative and positive revelations of herself in the immediate moment, but she is constantly aware that the child "is an independent subject and therefore rebellious; [he is] intensely real today, but in imagination [he is] the adolescent and adult of the future."[8] So, she may also respond to the child in terms of *imagined* possibilities, which may or may not have anything to do with present reality. I once heard parents describe their eight-year-old as "so selfish he'll never visit us at Christmastime once he's grown up." The boy wasn't especially mean; they were angry that he had just said something sassy, so his words fired their imagination. I have already been annoyed at my daughter for primping in front of a mirror because I had visions of her someday teasing her hair when she should be studying for exams. Another time I asked her a question and became upset when she didn't answer me right away. I interpreted her silence as surly teen-age behavior, proof she would grow up to ignore me. I was so caught up with my own pouting that it took me a few minutes to realize she was quiet because she didn't understand what one of my words meant. When I rephrased the question, we had a long, warm conversation.

It sounds confusing and complicated, and it is. You can never completely sort out all the forces influencing a father and mother in their relations with each other and their expectations of their children, just as a child's response to its parents is never "pure." But you *can* develop some awareness of your own "normal crazy" behavior and eventually help your child deal with similar inclinations to reshape the parents in her/his own likeness. Sometimes it helps to admit that Mommy is "acting a bit nervous today" because she is worried about something that she "can't put her finger on." Certainly you can better handle what is going on between you and your child if you can figure out some of the forgotten concerns that are surfacing in you again, and which may be coloring your perceptions of the child's behavior.

One way to handle these things is to prepare yourself for some of the reactions you are bound to have if you regard the child as an extension of yourself. Children learn by imitating and identifying with their parents, but hearing your favorite phrase being parroted by a three-year-old can be extremely embarrassing. You wonder why children always seem to latch onto your bad characteristics and not your good ones. After hearing my daughter shout out to her friends, "I'm telling you for the last time. . . ." I began to worry whether I was as bossy as she sounded. Not only did she sound like a shrew, but she spat out the words with her hands anchored on her hips in a look of disgusted resignation. It helps to remember that your own response to the child's behavior may be especially intense because you are reacting to the fact that the child has *exaggerated* your mannerisms in the course of trying them out.

A parent also needs to remember "that the way his or her child sees him depends by no means entirely on who or what he is. Rather it will depend very largely on what the child needs to have him be at any given time."[9] This insight can make things a little less confusing and complicated because it is good to remember that the child is *never* a static extension of the parent. The average child has contacts with both a mother and a father, siblings, neighbors, grandparents, cousins, and baby-sitters from the very beginning, so no *one* person is ever completely responsible for what the child absorbs. Besides, the child absorbs experiences according to her/his own independent needs. If the revelation of your "self" in the child is pleasing, be comforted. If the revelation of your "self" helps you to understand yourself better, profit by the opportunity. But do not take this "normal crazy" inclination so seriously that you hold yourself responsible for all the child's failings; that really *will* make you act crazy.

Another reaction mothers should be prepared for is how they will feel if the child actually is (or seems to be) more attractive, more intelligent, and more personable than the parent. You may delight in your ability to create a better model and enjoy the vicarious pleasure the success of someone near to you brings, but it can be awfully hard to live with someone who makes you look bad. The child's apparent success may make you feel more inadequate in an area you are already sensitive about. This reaction accounts for the father who wanted to give his son the professional education he did not have, but then snarled about "my educated son who thinks he is better than me, his old man." I wanted a beautiful daughter as proof of my own beauty, but I find myself resenting her firm, smooth flesh. I mutter that "Mommy is nothing but an old lady," hoping she will contradict me. I have a friend who yearned for an intelligent son and then spent hours worrying whether she was smart enough to take care of her precocious six-year-old: "In a few years there will be nothing he can learn from me; I won't be stimulating company for him." Not only can our responses to the failings we identify within the child be a trifle unhinged, but our responses to seeing our own possibilities realized in the child can be equally problematic. It helps to realize that identification and competition are first cousins. The child identifies with the parent, and the parent identifies with the child, but there is a constant tension—rich and stimulating though it is—in their appreciation of each other's uniqueness.

One reason for this tension is that "the parents love the children as their love, as the embodiment of their own substance,"[10] so they are unable to be comfortable with their children if they are not comfortable with themselves. And the truth is that most of us are *not* comfortable with ourselves. We keep expecting some ill-defined perfection in ourselves and in our children because they are supposed to be our second chance for perfection. Women have a special problem, because they have not been much encouraged to become clear about who and what they are, so they can tolerate the child's *separate identity*.* Women are often instructed to be "selfless" even before they have had a chance to develop a mature self-love. All too often, children have provided a woman with her *sole* identity.

Historically, women have been defined as loving others, and they have been warned against loving themselves too much or being narcissistic. But maybe they have decorated themselves with fancy jewelry, expensive perfumes, opulent furs, and other narcissistic ornaments only because the "self" that woman was left with by analysts was never very attractive without these disguises. In fact, woman was not even credited with much of a "self" to love. In 1821, Hegel said that woman is associated with "a life which

---

* A woman may face an extra dilemma if she receives signals from her husband, verbal or otherwise, requiring that his son or daughter do as well or better than he did: "Go to Harvard Law School, make the football team, do me proud," et cetera. Not only does such a mother have to deal with the child as part of herself, but she has to deal with the proprietary feelings of the father.

has not yet attained its full actualization"[11] because she functions "on the plane of feeling."[12] Women are like plants "because their development is more placid and the principle that underlies it is the rather vague unity of feeling."[13] Being compared to a plant and being told that a woman's life is incapable of full human actualization are not descriptions that encourage the development of self-confidence.

Hegel's pseudoscientific projection of his own prejudices is not without parallel in the last half of the twentieth century. Present-day talk of woman's "biological purpose," which requires "completion through conceiving," is an extension of the plant metaphor because it treats women as if flowering was their only function. Even though we may now smile at Hegel's dated language, it is still true that masculine goals urge men to do things, while femininity as an ideal *stops* women from doing them. It is no wonder that women who view themselves as amorphous, plantlike beings have difficulty with the notion that the child is kind of an extension of the parent. They find it difficult to tolerate a child who mimics them, because it seems like teasing, or the child who has skills that they do not have, because it points out their own wasted talents.

Let me quote again the mother in *Up the Sandbox*. Ann Roiphe accurately describes in this fictional character the personal worries of the thoughtful mother as she ruminates on her relationship with her daughter.

Is it something perhaps in the secret sticky protoplasm out of which I molded her—myself now devoted to a replica of myself, now slave, now master, caught in a bind. . . . What do I want from her when she grows up? Whatever it is, I am sure I won't get it. Whatever she will do will be less than what I have planned, because I can't help planning so much, asking so much of her. I always used to share the joke and point the finger at the ambitious stage mother, or the possessive Jewish mother whose son could not go to the bathroom without her following behind to wipe and admire his parts. And now I think those are visible caricatures of the even more sinister reality, the more ordinary poisonous ooze that flows between parent and child—Elizabeth is marred because she is mine and each waking hour I transmit in a thousand unconscious ways the necessary code for her to absorb my personality, to identify with my sex, and to catch, like a communicable plague, all my inadequacies and mimic them or convert them to massive ugly splotches on her own still young soul.[14]

Any chance for this mother to have developed a healthy self-love seems to have been sacrificed a long time ago on some primordial sexist altar. On an instinctual level, she realizes that her child will not mature if the mother does not love herself; she fears that the daughter will absorb all the self-hate she feels. The mother is tormented by her inadequacies, but she cannot put them into any sort of perspective. Like so many other intelligent mothers, this woman's sensitivity has prepared her to feel the despair of her role, but not to function in that interior place where the mutual identity problems of mother and child battle for attention. There is no shame in feeling proprietary, ambitious, and possessive. It is normal to want more of your children than they can give you, though it is important to stop yourself from stifling your children with these impulses.

Loving ourselves in a mature way is necessary if we are to love those reflections of ourselves, our children. When you can tolerate your own strengths and weaknesses with good humor (most of the time), then you are well on your way to coping with them in your children. Both sexes have problems with developing healthy self-confidence; it is easy to shortchange the "self" in our desire to avoid being selfish. But women have a cultural predicament reaching far beyond any personal troubles one might have in dealing with the tensions inherent in the conceptualization of the child as an extension of the parent. A mother is promised that children will fulfill her, so she is surprised, angry, and depressed when they seem as unsure of themselves as she is .These reflections of her own failings may further lower her self-esteem. Instead of questioning why she hoped her child would be the better part of her, she may be inclined to blame herself for not producing the miracle child.

To salvage some self-confidence, the mother may often try to order the ambivalences and frustrations she does not understand. It becomes more and more necessary for her to control her child's behavior, so she can comfort herself that she is a functioning adult. This is obviously unfair to everyone, for very little that is human flourishes under rigid controls. Understanding why we behave the way we do is what we need to work on.

Underneath all of the qualifications and demurrals, most middle-class, Spock-oriented mothers believe, deep in their hearts, that if they did their job well enough all of their children would be creative, intelligent, kind, generous, happy, brave, spontaneous, and good—each, of course, in his or her own special way.

—*Philip Slater*[1]

5

Being in Control

Somewhere along the line humans began to believe perfection was possible. What a sad day for mothers. Man became obsessed with the dream of a world of shared plenty; science would be married to philosophy, and the atom would become the great force for good (both physicists and moralists would be seated on white horses, of course). This new world would need some new people, and mothers were asked to deliver the goods. While fathers were out taming the universe, mothers were supposed to be taming their children. Since modern man was using the scientific method, softened by humanistic concern, to accomplish his task, modern woman was urged to be precise and well-informed, though kindhearted and intuitively sympathetic in her job. The more people learned about their physical and psychological world, the more there was to order, digest, utilize, and manipulate. Besides feeling disappointed because their children did not provide them with the promised personal fulfillment, mothers found themselves defined as the "focus of warmth and stability," yet chided for being neurotically emotional, and encouraged to raise children who would be both obedient and spontaneous.

After examining two centuries of child-rearing manuals, Samuel

Klausner said that if a parent were to try to follow all the recommendations in these books, child rearing would be an impossible task because the same manual might call for apparently contradictory behavior.[2] How true. And a quick survey of the popular and professional literature shows that "oughts" exist for everything: physical care, social development, instinctual satisfaction, moral education, need fulfillment, latent possibilities, cultural enhancement, and sexual gratification. Yet many of the new insights seem to contradict old facts. Or as Harding puts it, the "bad" mother is blamed for the child's difficulties, and the "good" mother is told that the child is now bound to her in an "inescapable fixation."[3]

What's a mother to do? First, she gets depressed because she is not like all those millions of ancient mothers who have "instinctively and intuitively known how to protect and raise children."[4] Then she starts to read all those how-to-do-it books. She becomes obsessed with how to speak "childrenese" at the breakfast table. She memorizes the 291 ways to amuse your child on a rainy day. She diligently fills out those quizzes in the Sunday magazine section that ask: "Are you a Good Mother?" Probably the taste for soap operas and advice columns arises because they seem to order emotions and conflicts.[5] In mothers' lives, schedules assume an importance that would confound men who earn a living by doing time and motion studies. Even schemas that were intended to be suggestive rather than dogmatic are utilized as iron-clad commandments to be displayed prominently on the refrigerator door. The mother plots out on paper the child's progress through the oral stage, latency, and puberty. Is the child trustful? Will autonomy, shame, or doubt win the day? On the child's second birthday, the mother practically cringes at the thought of living with the celebrated "terrible two." A sensitive mother can be so intimidated by all those "oughts"—from the ninety-eight pieces of clothing the average layette should contain to the thirty-two qualities that should be budding in the normal two-year-old—that she regularly has to fight the all-pervasive desire to be "in control" of the child every minute of the day.

It should come as no surprise that a mother who feels out of control because she can't get rid of her own negative feelings or ineffective in dealing with the reflection of her own failings in her children will try to forget her impotence by rigidly regulating her child's behavior. In that way, mothers are like some government agencies; they try to order the things they don't comprehend because there are too many pressures and variables to be adequately understood. Many of us mothers aspire to being in control the way our mothers seemed to be, or more likely, the way we wanted them to be. We keep responding to society's hope that the earth will turn into paradise if mothers will only produce a generation of totally satisfied individuals—orally-anally-genitally—poised and ready to be productive, social-minded citizens. (By the way, one wonders if an orally-anally-genitally satisfied individual wouldn't be paralyzed by complacent smugness.)

Deeply ingrained in American culture is the idea that if only we develop the right know-how, we can lick any problem. If we systematize and analyze behavior, we are bound to get the proper results. And if things go wrong, it's because we've done something wrong; we probably didn't have the proper ethical or mental set. We certainly act as if perfection is possible in both parents and children as long as we just accumulate enough knowledge. Actually, however, instead of producing the modern Renaissance woman, the knowledge explosion in this century has confused most mothers. They have been deluged with all sorts of seemingly contradictory theories about child rearing. Since distinguished journals have published these ideas, and most American women respect the appeal to authority, they have struggled to act on this advice without questioning any of the basic assumptions. There is in all of us a strong tendency to want to be modern and up-to-date, so we become disciples of whatever theories are enjoying book-club popularity. When every new behavioral insight is heralded as *the* answer to society's miseries, we become increasingly afraid of failing as a parent and less able to give the baby the casual, good-humored, loving care we are told that she/he needs. What is the answer? I do not know the complete answer, but it might help to offer mothers some casual, good-humored, loving attention. And with anything but perfection in mind, we might take a friendly look at the tendency to control ourselves and our children.

Control is a feature of mother-child relations even before the egg is fertilized. No matter what your ethical opinions on abortion and contraception are, you cannot help but feel that a large percentage of people prize deciding for themselves when they are going to become parents and how many children they will have. What used to be determined by the fates and the fertility of the partners is now controlled by man or, to be more accurate, by woman. There is more and more talk of ideal spacing and trying to influence what the sex of the offspring will be by using the appropriate acid or alkaline douche. Couples discuss when they will be "ready" for children and even whether they are suited temperamentally to having any children. Implicit in this talk is the dangerous notion that you can control the parent-child relationship if you only do the "right" thing.* Yes, Virginia, you too can be a success. (I appreciate parents' sensible attempts to understand experiences better by preparing for them, but so often we move from some casual ordering to rigid control, and it is this phenomenon I want to deal with here.) Of course, if you do not manage to deliver the child according to plan, during your husband's annual vacation, for instance, you may begin the whole relationship feeling inadequate. And if you can never decide when you will be ready to have a baby but just go off "the pill" to see what happens,

---

* Whatever one's views on the 1973 Supreme Court abortion ruling, on-demand abortion on the grounds that women should control their own bodies does reinforce the notion that the child is simply an extension of the mother. By asking for the power to decide for themselves which unborn babies should be carried to term, women are indirectly reaffirming the mother's control over the baby's life, as well as her own.

you may wind up feeling something of a failure from the very beginning.

It is easy to move from the thought that if you can control the circumstances of your baby's birth, you can control the baby's behavior later. It comes as quite a shock to parents that the fetus that can be aborted without legal recriminations at the age of three months, becomes in six short months a person with full rights of her/his own. Even if you do not feel like murdering your child soon after birth, you may occasionally wish that she or he would just go away. You are not sure you want to go through with it; then it hits you that society says this is a big "NO-NO." How and when did you lose control of your own destiny? Somewhere along the line the baby became a real person, no longer subject to your whims. I think even the mother who desperately wants to have a child has some difficulty realizing that from the moment of birth she is dealing with an *independent* being, not just a baby doll. This independent being that Simone de Beauvoir says "is defined and affirmed only in revolting against you"[6] may seem to be the exact opposite of the happy self-fulfillment you wanted. Having lost control of the baby's body, it becomes more and more necessary for the mother to be in control of her child's development, so she can comfort herself that she is a functioning adult.

No one expects to be able to blow a whistle and have the child go on happily to the next activity. But mothers expect to act in a controlled way themselves, because maturity is equated with being in control of one's emotions and impulses, and they expect to be able to shape the child into a really *outstanding product*.[7] Since women are educated in the competitive ways of our society and are indoctrinated with the idea of being on top, it is essential that their children be successful. We spend hours trying to do the "right" thing, but the "right" thing never seems to happen. We push our children in the direction of the ideal, only to find that we and they are anything but ideal. Impossible child-rearing ambitions manipulate us, and we respond by manipulating our children. We try to compartmentalize our own reactions and those of our children, because intelligent mothers should know what they are doing with their children.

By compartmentalizing I mean that we come up with all sorts of rules (usually ones that we never admit out loud) about what is appropriate. For example, I know that you are supposed to prepare a child for new experiences, so months ahead of time, I began talking to my daughter about the baby that was expected in the summer. We talked about mommies and daddies who had more than one child. We played games: "How many children do Mr. and Mrs. Barron have?" My daughter was supposed to get the idea that siblings are normal parts of families. We talked about how she would probably feel when the baby came home from the hospital; I encouraged her to express angry, aggressive feelings. We discussed what the baby would look like, what the baby would be able to do, and whether it would be a girl or a boy. I stressed the fact that infants cannot play games so my daughter would not be disappointed when the baby just lay there being demanding. In fact, we talked about how fussy babies are, that they are not as nice as little girls of three who can do things. But I also tempered this emphasis by mentioning that sisters and brothers grow up to be friends who keep each other company in the sandbox. I read my daughter stories about how chicks grow and how older children feel when a new baby puts in an appearance. I turned up the volume when Mr. Rogers sang, "When A Baby Comes to Your House," so that my daughter would get the idea that she "came before" and was special. This whole educational program (or propaganda campaign, depending on your viewpoint) was paced gradually so she would not feel that I was attaching too much importance to the baby. And when I went to the hospital, my three-year-old got a small present every day from Mommy and Daddy so she would not feel left out when the baby got presents and attention. I had even arranged for my two daughters to exchange gifts when they met for the first time as a sign of mutual welcome: the baby received a little plush lion from her sister, and my other daughter was presented with a *larger* lion. And so, after all this effort and preparation, why did my daughter suck her thumb and cling to her blanket in an especially obsessive way when she looked at the baby during those early weeks?

I felt like a failure. I must have done something wrong. Maybe I hadn't been appropriately understanding, flexible, informed, loving, disciplined, sympathetic, sensitive, or creative enough. Was I doing something to make her feel she *had* to react to the baby? Maybe I had drawn the wrong conclusions from child-rearing literature. Maybe my daughter is basically perverse. If she were at all decent and American, she would have been able, after all, to rise above sibling rivalry, wouldn't she?

It was only months later I realized mothers tend to blame themselves and their children if some absurd notion of perfection is not realized. Somehow, I had confused helping my child handle her reactions to a new experience with eliminating anything that even vaguely resembled a negative reaction. I let her feel angry before the baby's birth, but not afterward. In some magical way I hoped that kicking baby dolls before the baby's arrival would rid her forever of any desire to hit her new sister. I tried to organize her feelings into distinct compartments.

It is easy to confuse anticipating what makes a child normally feel upset with eliminating the upset completely. If negative reactions can be minimized, isn't it possible for supermother to banish them all together? Isn't this one of the goals that mothers are supposed to have? Read the experts and that's the impression you get, since mothers are chastized for the child's every imperfection.

R. D. Laing put into words the awesome responsibility mothers feel when he said that they "are always the first to get the blame for everything."[8] Mothers have been blamed for schizophrenia and birth deformities (what frightened the mother was thought to leave its mark on the unborn child), for barren environments and the content of their children's dreams. Wars might disappear if mothers would only encourage their children to be even-tempered and generous! Pamphlets announce: "Caring for the baby is the most important job in your life . . . any faltering or laxity on your part will have consequences on the future well-being of your child."[9] Humans are supposed to flourish for a lifetime if they get the right cuddling and caring in their first six years, so women are ordered to bathe the child in love just as they surrounded the fetus with amniotic fluid *in utero.*

If they are "adequate" females, they are supposed to be able to meet the needs of the child as spelled out by psychiatrists, pediatricians, and priests. *Instinctively,* they are supposed to know how to nurture, comfort, and encourage self-control. The mother is responsible if the child isn't cheerful and sensitive to others, considerate yet able to protect herself/himself, dependable but independent, mannerly and exuberant, popular but unselfish. Booklets that raise the question "Is there an ideal mother?" and then deny that such a person exists always manage to leave you with the definite impression that perfection is possible if only you try hard or stop trying so hard. Thousands of behavioral objectives have been expected of mothers because of their magic maternal hormones. Spurred on by the experts who idealize children, mothers struggle for an impossible control over feelings, behavior, and reactions in themselves and in their children. They are too guilty to admit that some of the child rearing advice might have as much substance as the Emperor's new clothes.

When I speak critically of control, I do not question parents' responsibility for developing impulse control in themselves and in their children. I do not approve of children who settle differences by throwing sand in each other's eyes or parents who tear up a child's notebook just because the lettering is sloppy. There are appropriate and inappropriate ways to handle feelings and impulses, and both children and parents should work toward behaving in a constructive way in their dealings with each other. What I am concerned about is that so much of what gets described as "appropriate" is often not very realistic. Unfortunately, we usually confuse the appropriate with the ideal without really knowing it.

We rarely question why a specific action is defined as appropriate or what alternative behavior is open to us. In fact, ordering our world often takes precedence over understanding the human experience. A good example of this is when your child first goes to nursery school.

Mothers who value nursery school are usually eager to have two or three mornings a week to themselves (or with their younger children). They are also eager to give their children a chance to play with others of the same age. Most mothers try to prepare their children for the new experience, anticipating some trouble in the first week or two when the child realizes Mother will eventually be leaving her/him in the company of strangers. Nursery schools usually require the mother to stay around the first week so the child can get used to new surroundings while still seeing a friendly, familiar face. Some may even expect the mother to stay around "until the child is ready for the separation." This all sounds so sensible. The child will be able to derive satisfaction from new stimuli gradually, and the mother can feel good about encouraging independence and socialization in a flexible kind of way. This scenario would be wonderful if only it worked out, but it rarely does in the way we want it to, at least in my experience. Both nursery school teachers and parents tend to confuse their idea of the appropriate with the ideal. Just because provision has been made for handling a new situation with flexibility, it doesn't follow that in two weeks' time the result will be a child perfectly adjusted to nursery school. You may be saying to yourself, "I don't expect perfection, so what's the problem?" The problem is that while we know children are individuals who rarely do what they are supposed to do (in this case, be adjusted to nursery school in two weeks' time), we still somehow expect that they will, and react strongly when they do not. We want to control the new experience with *"flexible"* methods, but we get terribly angry when we cannot control the results. Being informed parents, we have learned to anticipate regression and distemper in our children, but we have very definite, rigid ideas about what is permissible fussiness and exactly how long it should last. We confuse *knowing* more about behavior with *controlling* behavior more effectively. And if things don't work out according to plan, we want to blame someone—probably the mother.

When it comes to nursery school, all too often neither parents nor teachers question their basic assumptions. Since everyone expects the child to have some negative feelings about a strange new experience, why is everyone so upset when a child actually is naughty? Does it really help to have nervous mothers sitting on the sidelines while their skittish children try to figure out what is going on? If your child doesn't enjoy nursery school, does it mean that she/he is not college material? What does it mean for a child to be ready for separation from the mother? Do separation feelings bloom only in the first two weeks, or can't they develop halfway through the school year? What about the mother whose child does not seem to miss her? After all, tears are considered the norm for the first couple of weeks. Why do adults always want feelings to last only so long and then be gone completely? Why do mothers feel they have failed when their children cry? How do parents' feelings about making new friends, or thoughts about what it means for the child to be independent, influence the whole adjustment period? Why do mothers feel guilty when they want their children to go to nursery school instead of wanting them to stay at home all day? These questions may not be the ones you would want to ask, but in order to cope effectively, we must question what is considered appropriate, desirable, or ideal. What do you want to control in your child so you won't have to feel guilty or disappointed? Not that you have to analyze every action, but it certainly helps to ask, "Why did I do that?" "Why was I so disappointed when she did that?"

I know that I find myself trying to regulate my feelings and my child's behavior all the time. I set aside "do special things with the five-year-old time" and continue to be disappointed when she doesn't feel like doing anything special. I read that demand feeding makes sense with the newborn because it conforms to the infant's real needs; the baby will probably grow into a regular three-or-four-hour schedule after the first few weeks. Imagine my annoyance when my two children never did regularize their demands. I want my children to be creatively messy and compulsively neat at the times I designate. I disapprove of children being forced to keep their noses to the academic grindstone, but I want my daughters to be smart, though personable and lots of fun. In short, I want them to be brilliant, yet never look like drudges. I want my children to enjoy their bedrooms, but I resent it when they move the furniture around, destroying the harmony of their rooms with piles of toys and dirty clothes. I want them to be independent, but only in areas where I can tolerate their wills challenging my own. I want my children to be sensitive to the needs of others and to what is going on inside of them, but never to express their sensitivity by whining or sobbing. I expect my children to be happy at Christmas, even though there has always been something about holiday time that makes me melancholy. I resent it when my daughter says, "Is that all?" after ripping through a huge stack of presents, even though I have always wanted "more."

These examples may sound like the confessions of a "compulsive" mother. I readily admit my compulsions, but I think that my own tendency to want to order experiences accurately reflects all mothers' general tendency to want to package reactions in cellophane wrap so they will be supermarket-neat and unobtrusive. And the more that child-rearing literature talks about maternal responsibilities without talking about the *"normal* crazy" thoughts and feelings that go along with being a parent, the more we internalize literally insane expectations for ourselves and our children. After all, expectations about behavior and achievement are a form of coercion. Psychologically, we coerce ourselves (and our children) every time we have an expectation. An expectation can be a friendly push toward a desired goal, or it can be a form of torture.

I have often wondered if the importance we attach to ordering experiences does not account in part for so many people's picture-taking obsessions. On more than one occasion, I have noticed that slides, movies, and pictures of vacations or family events often seem to satisfy in a way the event itself did not. The picture of the huge, old-fashioned family gathered together for an annual picnic may bring more joy than the actual party. We keep hoping for family relations completely free of tensions and quarrels, so we pretend that the photograph, with its many smiling faces, is the reality. It might be a good deal more pleasant in the long run if we took a look at those expectations that interfere with reality. Mind you, analysis cannot make things perfect, but it might help us learn to live with imperfection. We are inclined to like things better after the fact. Halcyon days are usually those remembered, not the ones that we live through in the present. Wouldn't it be healthier to try to live with our every-day ambivalences than to decorate the past in order to have a piece of our lives resemble our crazy expectations? If we do not come to terms with real thoughts and feelings, we may find ourselves loving eight-by-ten pictures more than our children.

We cannot end this discussion of a mother's "normal crazy" obsession with being "in control" without asking, "What are we so busy controlling?" By now the answer should be apparent. We are trying to control the contradictions we see in ourselves and our children. We are trying to reconcile the common attitude of contempt for women and the respect shown for mothers. All of us struggle personally with the myth of female weakness (which preaches subordination to man) and the myth of female power (woman as the giver of life). Woman has the power to create a child and mold her/him into a social being, yet child rearing traditionally demands self-sacrifice, even a certain self-immolation. Women are defined by men as beneficent givers. They are dominated by male-authored visions of the "happy" and "adjusted" child, demanding more than any human being can give. Mothers are seen as omnipotent by young children, because they magically produce presents or spank with the fury of a sudden summer thunderstorm, yet they are often dependent on their children for worldly status. Mothers are responsible for everything that goes wrong, but they are taken for granted when things go right.

We feel these contradictions every day, so we feverishly try to structure a world where the real and the ideal, the appropriate and the inappropriate will not be so far apart. We are trying to live in that emotional space where opposites are the force of life. We try to control our aggressive feelings and those of our children so as not to feel threatened by them. And we are mortally afraid that the aggression of the mother, carefully buried beneath layers of an inherited, perhaps mythical, altruism, might be more terrible if unleashed on our trusting dependents than anything a man ever felt. So we rigorously control what we are too scared to name in our personal lives.

What do I suggest in the place of some crazy notion of being "in control?" I suggest that we start thinking the unthinkable, start feeling the unfeelable. Mothers should give a name to the contradictions they feel. Instead of putting artificial restrictions on a child's behavior, maybe we should think out loud (spouse to spouse) about what we are really afraid of. (It's the attitudes parents attach to certain acts and gestures of their children that frighten them, yet these assumptions may or may not be true.) Are we afraid that if we do not holler at our son every time he whines, he will grow up to be a sissy? Are we afraid that the four-year-old daughter who wiggles her bottom in front of strangers will be a whore on Times Square in twelve more years? Are we afraid that our three-year-old will turn into a spaced-out, heroin-shooting monster by the age of thirteen if we do not do something about his present addiction to chocolate ice cream? Are we afraid that the daughter who stomps her foot when she is angry will hurl dishes and obscenities at us in a few years if we do not eradicate her present unbecoming behavior? Are we afraid that if we spank our two-year-old son when he has been obnoxious, he will wind up seeing all women as castrating bitches? Are we afraid that meeting a child's demands will make him all the more demanding? Are we afraid to get angry because we are worried that we will not be able to stop feeling ferocious and not be able to handle those demons locked inside of us?

No matter how silly or terrible your concerns seem, once you say them out loud, they are there ready to be dealt with. Think about what you are afraid of, evaluate how reasonable it is to think and feel that way. It is better to name a real worry than to live saddled with anxiety that knows no name. See if you cannot think of some way to experiment with new, more constructive behavior. You will be lucky to find "solutions" to a small percentage of your worries, but regularly trying to name what is bothering you will make you feel more grown up and less constrained. If you are concerned over the fact that you "spank when mad," and find yourself peppering the air with verbal lashings in a determined attempt not to lay a hand on your child, becoming clear about your worries may make you feel more capable. Then you might think about the fact that you are a very "physical" person, who hugs and kisses when happy, but who also feels like slapping flesh when fired up. How old is the child? What seems appropriate punishment for this age? Does the child seem to understand that spankings are part of the "mad you," just as caresses are part of the "loving you," or does she/he tremble with fear each time you get a little bit angry? When are spankings most effective? Is your verbal abuse worse than a short spanking? Do you feel like pushing the child around because you feel "pushed around?" Clearly, there is no *right* answer. You probably will never ask yourself all these questions at the same time, but eventually you may develop a more realistic notion of what "better" might mean in this particular situation (and "better" does not mean perfect).

In fact, deciding which is better—to spank or to holler—is not just your problem. The child is part of the problem, so why can't she/he be part of the solution? Over lunch one day, I asked my older daughter what she thought she should do when Mommy is angry, and she answered, "The Mommy's child should ask the Mommy why she is so mad." I asked her if she preferred to be asked "What's the matter?" when she is angry or whether she'd rather scream and hit. And she responded, "Of course, I want my Mommy to ask what's the matter; that's why I'm bad in the first place." (Mind you, she usually isn't this precocious.) Perhaps what my daughter expressed is in fact the goal. Parents and children should both get used to saying out loud what is bothering them (*and* what makes them happy) and to encouraging each other in this direction. Instead of control, with all its static connotations, you have reciprocal movement and growth.

You try to encourage understanding in the child: "I'm not mad at you, but reading all the terrible and sad things in the newspaper has made Mommy feel rotten." It has to work both ways. You try to understand the child: "Do you cry every time I kid you because you don't like me to laugh at you, and you don't understand what I think is so funny?" or "Do you sometimes find it hard to stop crying once you start crying?" It is important for parents and children to be clear about what they find disappointing, depressing, overwhelming, and frightening, and to talk about these things with each other, so that both generations can have day-to-day proof that no one is perfect. The mother can talk about her worries: "Why are you always angry with Mommy when things don't go right?" "Why do you listen to me when I scream and not when I talk quietly?" And the child can verbalize her/his concerns: "Does kindergarten mean I'll have to learn how to read right away?" "Will I have to grow up if I don't want to?" "Do you know how hard it is to be good *all* the time?"

As parents we have to come to terms with our imperfect selves and our imperfect world and try to find more constructive ways of maximizing our own potential and our children's. We have to be able to name the personal and cultural contradictions that dry up creative relationships between the generations. Thus far, I have pointed out how expectations influence our functioning as mothers. I have analyzed how certain "normal crazy" feelings, impulses, and reactions, which are usually ignored in the child-oriented literature, can point the way to growth and development in the parent. Now, let us consider a specific period that each child goes through, in which the mutual influence of developing parents on developing children can be scrutinized: the Oedipal-Electra period. The mother learns something about herself in each phase that the child goes through, but the period from three to six is especially important, because that's when children start asking you what it means to be a woman and a mother.

Once upon a time, when Jack was little,
he wanted to be with his mummy all the time
and was frightened she would go away
later, when he was a little bigger,
he wanted to be away from his mummy
and was frightened that
she wanted him to be with her all the time.

—R. D. Laing[1]

6

And How Did Jocasta Feel?

Did you ever wonder how Jocasta felt when she had to give up Oedipus, her son, to a shepherd, to be abandoned on a mountain to die, because of the prophecy that Oedipus would kill his father and marry his mother? She probably had a hard time feeling kindly to a son with such naughty inclinations, and to her husband, Laius, who believed the worst of his son. Poor mother, poor father; after trying so hard to do the right thing, the inevitable happened. The child was given instead to the king of another country, killed his father in a quarrel, and, in return for solving a riddle, was given the queen, his mother, as wife. When he finally learned the truth, he blinded himself as punishment, and his mother hanged herself.[2] Before exploring the developmental issues, supposedly personified by Oedipus and Electra (a girl who had murderous feelings about her mother), I cannot help wondering if all parents don't have some friends who warn them to expect the worst in their children. Aren't you always inclined to have unkind thoughts and feelings when you think trouble is inevitable, especially when you have tried so hard to do the right thing? Did Laius accuse Jocasta of being too seductive with Oedipus as a toddler? What was Jocasta's reaction when Laius said the best way to handle a troublesome child is to get rid of him? Are all children destined to be punished for unknown wrongs and to be the death of their parents? It is hard to imagine what these mythic personalities thought and felt, but I find it fascinating to wonder what everyday themes this story contains besides the one Freud emphasized.

My whimsical speculations are aimed primarily at underlining the fact that no one ever mentions the parents' point of view in this famous story. And, except for occasional pronouncements about the attitude one ought to have about masturbation and sex education, no one discusses the child's Oedipal-Electra period (or phallic stage, or beginning of psychosexual development, as it is sometimes called) from the parents' point of view. This phase between the ages of three and six encompasses the child's discovery of pleasurable sensations in the genitals, as well as the child's attraction to the parent of the opposite sex.

At this age children want to know "how things work" and how their bodies function. They are fascinated by what it means to have a special relationship, as their mothers and fathers have, with a beloved person. Naturally, they envy their parents who sleep together, fighting off loneliness and bad dreams side-by-side. Children want to have some guarantee that they will never be alone, friendless, and unloved, so they wish for the closeness of marriage (even angry togetherness may seem better than being isolated in a room that gets dark at night). They are also eager to experiment with self-gratification. They already know what they like to eat, whether a blanket or a thumb is more soothing, and what it is like to relax on someone's lap when they are tired. Of course, some of this behavior may be criticized at this point as babyish, so they keep looking around to see how adults relax and enjoy themselves.

As they look around, they usually wish (perhaps not out loud) that they had a husband or a wife (if you cannot act like a baby, they figure, you might as well act like a grownup), and if the child is a girl she may resent her mother's good luck in having her father for a husband, just as the boy resents his father. Being angry does not seem to help, so the child usually resolves her/his feelings by trying to be more and more like the parent of the same sex, who seems to be getting all the attention the child wants. The little girl figures that if she can grow up to be like her mommy, she can get a husband like her daddy. And the boy imitates his father's behavior so he can be "man" enough for his mother to feel for him what she feels for her husband.

Much has been written about these normal thoughts and feelings of the child, though I have never quite understood why such a gory and unnatural story as Oedipus's adventures should have become equated with this period in the child's development. Freud may have wanted to shock Victorian parents out of the pastel, candied atmosphere of the "children's hour" into realizing that their children could have murderous, jealous feelings, but the tactics he used have also scared several generations of parents into feeling totally inadequate with their four-year-old Lolita and Portnoy. My primary purpose in this chapter, however, is not to criticize the unnatural tale that analysts have used to point out *natural* behavior, but instead to explore an important period of the child's growing up as it relates to the parents' growing up. Specifically, I want to explore the parent's "normal crazy" thoughts, feelings, impulses, and fantasies as she or he deals with (1) the sexual interests of the child; (2) the child's attraction for the parent of the opposite sex; and (3) the child's identification with the parent of the same sex. (Though my emphasis will continue to be on the mother-daughter relationship, it should be clear from my examples that both parents have similar reactions to their sons and daughters during this developmental stage.)

All of us have some notion that touching the genitals, giggling about standing or sitting to urinate, worrying about whether something is missing (be it a penis, developed breasts, or a womb), and wanting to know where babies come from are part of the preschool child's behavior. There is usually no mention, though, that this behavior quite normally reawakens old memories in the parent.

Oh, there may be some talk that a father who is ambivalent about his own sexual behavior may saddle his son with his own neurotic fears or that the frigid woman will blow a cold wind in her child's direction and freeze all those normal impulses for life, or at least until the psychiatrist thaws them out again. But the notion that the developmental concerns of the child *always* precipitate some re-thinking on the part of the parent is ignored because she/he presumably is grown up and need not rethink anything. (Rethinking is usually equated with having done something wrong the first time, which needs correcting, rather than with movement and growth as it should be.) What form this rethinking takes varies from parent to parent, but I know that my five-year-old's interest in herself as a sexual person has made me think about myself as a sexual person.

You have only to watch your child's struggles with coming to terms with her/his body to realize how unsatisfactorily you as an adult have come to terms with your body. How many of us like what we see in the mirror? Are we too tall or too short? Is the nose too pointy or too squat? Is the hair too stringy or too frizzy? Are the legs too skinny or too fat? Is the penis smaller or bigger than average? Are the breasts pendulous like an old woman's, or do they look more like two forlorn pimples? If you are like me and have fantasized about magically turning into a divine, voluptuous, superdesirable woman, panted after by every man, you might begin to hope that your daughter will never feel that she has to "be-come" beautiful. Instead, you may decide that helping her get through this period means helping her realize that her body al-ready is special. She does not have to wait to be special, nor does she have to wait to be defined as beautiful by someone else. Beautiful is when you love your own body enough to live in harmony with it.

I don't want to sound like a deodorant commercial, but confi-dence is beauty. The slogan "Black is beautiful" is a good example of how coming to terms with yourself can bring the existing values for what is beautiful into question. The self-confident person can convince us that what she/he has is beautiful. In effect, every child should be encouraged to think, "Prove to me I am not special and beautiful," rather than be shunted into a competitive world that emphasizes values someone else is supposed to have. (The usual putdown of this kind of thinking is that children raised this way would be conceited. But then "conceited" has been tied up with stereotyped thinking that assumes if you value yourself, you cannot value anyone else, especially if that person looks different from the way you do.) Once you begin to think in terms of living in harmony with your body, you have some chance of helping your child deal with the question of whether her/his body is attractive and well made. I would be a liar if I left you with the impression that thinking about these issues transformed me and my daughter into self-assured paragons of femininity in only eight weeks. But figuring out what she is going through and simultaneously thinking about my uneasiness in the same area have made me feel more able to deal with her needs. I am also beginning to think that the "desirable" woman I dreamed of becoming belongs in a sexist film and not in my fantasy world. (And my husband has come to appreciate the arch of his cheekbones and his one-sided dimple without getting bogged down in whether they are "manly.")

When I watch my daughter stroke the silky binding of her blanket in a blatantly erotic fashion, I cannot help wondering whether all the adults who have mastered the complexities of sexual intercourse have forgotten to enjoy themselves as sensual creatures in the process of developing mechanical proficiency. We tend to equate the Oedipal-Electra period with the awakening of specific genital curiosity and behavior, but we forget that it is also the time for learning that *the body is generally sensuous*. Eyes were made for looking at scarlet-colored balloons; hands were made for fondling velvety fabrics; bodies were made for dressing up in exotic outfits and for covering with warm sand. Watching my daughter and her friends take such sybaritic pleasure in life has reminded me that I have denied my own sensuous nature. My daughter has to learn the conventions that I already know, but I find myself relearning what it means to be sensuous and indulge in the pleasures of sounds, colors, tastes, and beautiful shapes. I have tried to recapture some sense of spontaneity in what I do, say, think, and feel, and to become more pleasure-oriented in how I structure my day. My daughter reintroduced me to the soothing luxury of a bubble bath and to the charms of reading out loud and pretending. Her expressiveness has encouraged my own. I find the edges of my personality rounding out, not because she has fulfilled me, but because her own sensuous, spontaneous, pleasurable self is a good role model.

Because she has qualities that I can appreciate and even want to emulate does not mean that she does not have a good deal to learn. To be aware of the body means that you have to discover what is satisfying to the senses and tension-reducing, but also socially acceptable. Both daughters love to snuggle with favorite stuffed animals, to wrap themselves into a snug blanket cocoon, and to satisfy their mouths with rhythmic in-and-out thumb movements. But is my five-year old getting too big to go around with blankets and toys and a thumb stuck in her mouth? Should I deny her these satisfactions in the name of growing up? Deep down, I am afraid that she may go job hunting, her thumbs still sore from sucking. I guess I also feel uncomfortable just thinking about the sexual meaning of her mouth needing to have something in it. Does she need to cling to babyish satisfactions because her body is changing and she does not know how to respond in any other way? I think of what behavior to offer her in place of these habits. I prefer thumb sucking to masturbating or overeating. In thinking these thoughts, I have gained new understanding of why I should not embarrass or threaten her out of old behaviors, for she is caught between being a baby and a big girl. I resent that she is not a "satisfied" child all the time, yet I also have more sympathy for her and my own needs. I think of what will relax her: discussing her worries and feelings, diverting her with games and stories, encouraging expressive activities—finger painting, making Jello, dancing to loud music, making her laugh and giggle—hugging and kissing her when she is sad or happy. And I have begun to think that thirty-year-old mothers have a tremendous need for diversions and expressive activities, for the satisfied mother may be the biggest tension reducer you can offer the child. I have come to reappreciate how soothing kneading bread, raking leaves, scrubbing floors (if you don't have to do them too often), and throwing snowballs can be for me.

Although my daughter's emergence as a sexual person has encouraged me to rethink what it means to be beautiful, sensuous, and satisfied, her beginning awareness of her body's potential has brought me, most of all, into a head-on confrontation with my own ambivalence about sexual matters. She looks at my big breasts while I am taking a bath and wrinkles her nose at the thought of her lean body ever being burdened by such protrusions. I remember how I used to pray that I would never develop breasts, because I thought I wouldn't be able to walk down the street if I had so much weight in such an unlikely place. How could you breathe with those funny things wobbling in front of you? But then, I also wondered how boys could walk without a penis getting in the way of free movement. My daughter wonders out loud if she is going to get hair under her arms, and I remember fears of turning into a boy, or maybe an animal, once I developed pubic hair and a furry growth on my legs. When my daughter says, "I think that girls are softer and prettier than boys," memories of endless debates with myself about whether my mother or my father was more attractive become reactivated.

Then and now, I still wonder if the young child's body is not more lovely and lovable than that of the full-blown woman. I am not unlike the mother who admires the promise of sexuality more than mature reality.

I called her for her bath. I helped her undress and splashed the water for her and soaped the park dirt off. I looked at her small body, a vagina so smooth and hidden, the tiny clitoris still white, like a marble statue, so unlike my hairy mound, so unlike my full labia and the pulsating, discharging, odorous, membranous opening, scarred by two episiotomies (a slight scar—I needed a magnifying mirror to notice it). If I looked very closely I could see the soft blond fuzz on Elizabeth's mound that would one day grow thick and bushy, covering the oozy changes that would go on below. I felt sad somehow that we couldn't preserve the sculptured perfection of our own immature genitals.[3]

I appreciate my daughter's schizophrenic reasoning that the little girl and the woman are different creatures, not related to each other despite their sharing of the same suit of skin. I weep for what I was and am. Yet I am beginning to love my past, my present, and future because the connections that I make for her—between what she was and what she is, between what she is and what she will be—fasten me together. I listen to my daughter talk about having ten babies and then, five minutes later, scream that she does not want to have any babies. She looks in the mirror at the two pink dots that foretell a busty future and pulls them, shouting, "Those breasts aren't coming out today" with exuberant pleasure. She wants . . . she doesn't want. I reassure her that she will become grown up only when she is ready to be grown up, and yet I realize that I am not ready myself. This ambivalent tug and push brings us closer together, and yet we are becoming more and more separate.

I understand the extent of my own ambivalence when I find myself taking such pleasure in her genital interest. Her dreams of "having cocktails with a snake" amuse me. When she thrusts a big red towel between her legs and says, "See, I have the biggest penis in the world," her boldness makes me feel a vicarious thrill. When she stalks her father on his way to the shower to see what his penis looks like, I enjoy seeing a little girl making a grown man feel so awkward. But when she says, "I just had a silly thought; I was thinking what it would be like to take a nap with Uncle Phil," I feel uncomfortable. Since I find Uncle Phil attractive, I begin to wonder if I am egging her on in some unknown way to act out my libidinal fantasies. I listen to other parents take obvious pleasure in recounting how sexy their five-year-olds are, and I feel better. I comfort myself that it is terribly normal to enjoy your own child saying something saucy. Lusty inclinations in my child make me feel more lusty and alive, but, then again, I wonder if it would not be better to get my pleasure from bawdy Shakespearean ballads than to react to my child's behavior with giggles and enjoyment. Perhaps I am reinforcing behavior that is better sublimated or repressed. But, then again, I like giggling. And so it goes—thinking and feeling, reacting and evaluating, questioning and understanding—she grows and I grow.

One moment I kiss her as if she were a frisky puppy; then I feel self-conscious about my caresses because she is beginning to look more and more like a woman. I murmur endearments the way a lover would, and then I become aware of the possessive tone that can prevent rather than nurture her development. (I am sure that mothers of sons go through the same thing.) I help her to handle her feelings by making up stories—about a little girl who was scared because she thought she once had had a penis that was cut off by a bad witch, about a little girl who was afraid that she would turn into a bear once she grew pubic hair, about a little girl who worried that she would grow a penis and turn into a boy. We talk about how silly and scary it was for that mythical girl to have such crazy thoughts, and sometimes she even confides that she once thought that way herself. Helping her, I help myself. I find myself better able to distinguish between being affectionate and being seductive; I am learning to touch and soothe without being cloying. I learn to walk the tightrope between repression and indulgence, tolerance and control, gratification and restraint. And she learns, too.

Let's talk about the effect that the child's attraction to the father can have on the mother. I find it revealing that my first draft of the last sentence read "Let's talk briefly" about this. I think my inclination to want to be brief is symptomatic of how one parent feels when a child romances the other parent. You feel jealous, hurt, left out, angry, and depressed, and then, naturally, guilty, because of all these mixed-up feelings. You usually hope that they will go away if you do not think about them too much.

When I say the child is attracted to the parent of the opposite sex, I mean that the child is fascinated by what the other sex looks like grown up. "Do men pee-pee standing up like little boys do?" "Why do men have beards, and women don't?" "Why do men never wear dresses?" "Why do men's breasts never pop out?" "Do men take showers, rather than baths?" The child is interested in figuring out what makes men attractive in one way and women attractive in another way. They sense, I think, that men and women have a mysterious, secret relationship to each other that they do not understand but want to be a part of.

Children, at this point, often have some difficulty dealing with both parents at the same time. They can relate to one at a time, but they get furious if the parents are more interested in talking to each other over a late-afternoon drink than to their four-year-olds. It can be maddening to have your first moments together after a long work day interrupted by "Did you know, Daddy, that Mommy broke a glass while she was washing it?" Even if you realize that this obnoxious challenging behavior means that the child is growing up and is making some attempt to socialize with adults, you may resent the fact that she picked this moment to assert her individuality. Doesn't she know children are supposed to act like children and play with their toys, while the adults act like adults? Why does she act charming at six o'clock when Daddy comes home, when she acted like a spoiled brat during the eight hours before?

I consider myself an intelligent woman; I am prepared for my daughter to be intrigued by her father. I expect her to want to act grown up as she in fact grows up. I expect her to practice different ways of acting with her parents. I expect her to want to have a special relationship with each of us and sometimes to resent the special relationship that the adults have with each other. But I find I do not like it when she acts out some of these expectations! I never seem to be ready for this kind of behavior. When she fondles my husband's tie and musses his hair, I feel left out, jealous, and unwanted. Doesn't she know she is supposed to be the solace of my old age? Why can't everyone just have a special relationship with me? Why did she have to grow up so fast? Just when I was getting used to her babyish ways, why did she have to become so coy, so seductive, such a tease?

I resent it when she compliments my husband—"Daddy, I love your ties, your shirts, your pants, and your body"—yet I am pleased she is beginning to realize men are attractive (an important lesson) and that she can make a man feel wanted and loved. So I compliment her on being interested enough in another person to say something to make him feel happy. When she says, "I want something to happen which I know won't happen, but I want it anyway. I wish Daddy would take me on his next business trip so I could sleep with him in his bed," her words make me feel uncomfortable, but I like the fact that she can distinguish between what can be and what she wants. And I reassure myself that my articulate little girl is expressing a normal desire to take her mother's place; it doesn't mean she is turning into a nymphomaniac. She just realizes that having a person by your side is more comforting than having a bed full of stuffed animals and dolls.

In my more paranoid moments I am positive that my husband prefers my daughter to me.* Does he think that her trim figure is more appealing than my own? Is she wiggling her cute bottom just to annoy me? I resent her youth, her energy, her possibilities. I resist the ultimate fantasy, but still it hounds me: Will she steal my husband away from me? I do not like what I think; I do not like what I feel. I worry that I will turn into the kind of mother who tries to get even with her daughter by deliberately being seductive to all her daughter's boy friends. How I resent her possibilities!

* Fathers go through the same thing with their sons. The son fondles his mother's breasts while hugging her or strokes her hair, and the man feels jealous. There are times when the father worries that the child understands his wife's moods better than he does. All too often, the son compliments the mother on a new dress before the husband notices what she's wearing.

She still has the thrill of falling in love for the first time ahead of her. I know that I still have some thrills ahead of me, but I have so many happy moments *behind* me. She has such promise; I represent promise realized. But I do not feel realized and developed; yet I do. This fictional character expresses my own wonderings exactly:

I wonder, if I were Penelope, if I should not have smuggled myself aboard the ship originally headed for Troy. Or if perhaps, even now, I should not accept the hot kisses of some impatient suitor who would rape me on the hills and carry me off to a different city where the language itself would be unknown to me. I'm no Penelope, no romantic heroine or creature of historical importance. I'm just Margaret Reynolds, wife and mother, not yet thirty . . . too old for an identity crisis and yet not past the age of uncertainty.[4]

I am a real wife and mother, already thirty, and I know I am not too old for an identity crisis and that I will probably never get past the age of uncertainty. In fact, my daughter's uncertainty and search for identity make me more aware of my own. I am jealous of her now, but, most of all, of her future.

I am scared that I will become more and more like the woman Simone de Beauvoir describes:

The older the child gets, the more does resentment gnaw at the mother's heart; each year brings her nearer her decline, but from year to year the young body develops and flourishes; it seems to the mother that she is robbed of this future which opens before her daughter. . . . In contrast with the repetition and routine that are the lot of the older woman, this newcomer is offered possibilities that are still unlimited: it is these opportunities that the mother envies and hates; being unable to obtain them for herself, she often tries to decrease or abolish them.[5]

Will I turn into a mean, revenging shrew? Will I deliberately pull my daughter's long blonde hair every time I comb it? Will I start mocking her and making fun of her more and more? Or maybe I can dazzle her with my even disposition and understanding heart.

It should be obvious at this point that the child's behavior brings out feelings in the parent which point the way to how unfinished her/his own growing up is. I think that *all* parents have to rethink what it means to have a special relationship with someone, to want to be seen as special. We all have to deal with the fact that some of our possibilities have never been realized, some of our own promise has never been fulfilled. What does it mean when parents are jealous and envious of the generation they sired?* How can they handle these feelings? Can the more crazy aspects of this kind of competition be avoided? How can the normal ambivalence in parent-child relations be dealt with constructively?

And there is a large amount of ambivalence to deal with. The mother who delights in looking at her child's body is also the woman who is jealous of the future that that body has (whether the child is a boy or a girl). The child who says "I like you a thousand," because that is the highest number she knows, is also the daughter who says, "I dreamed that Mommy died last night, and me and my sister had our friends over, and we all took care of Daddy." She loves you, but she tells you that you "cooked a stinking meal," "read a lousy story," and that "you're not as pretty as I am because your teeth are yellowish and mine are very white." She hugs you as if you were the most vital force in her life; then she hits you in the breasts and says, "Yucky." (The equivalent for boys is to stage mock gun battles when the villain father comes home at 6 P.M., and say, "I take better care of Mommy than you do because I'm with her all the time," and kick father in the groin "by mistake" when they are splashing each other at the beach.) But even if parent and child are dealing with what looks like the

---

* This resentment of the older generation for the younger generation of the same sex is of great historical importance. Parents have always tended to be stern and judgmental when they see children of one sex being seductive toward adults of the other sex. Fantasies that the child will be able to steal the parent's love object become activated, and the adult wants to keep the child in an unprivileged limbo as long as possible. So the child will not take the place of the parent, old men have made wars in distant lands for young men to fight, the irrepressible spirit of youth has been subdued by the "school of hard knocks" obsession, and sexual curiosity has been curbed by the hatred felt for "loose morals."

same feelings, they have different developmental needs. The parent has to deal with the unfinished business of her/his maturing; the child has to deal with the basic business of growing up.

Some of a parent's negative feelings about the child may be resolved when the child reaches the point where she/he identifies with the parent of the same sex, but identification with the parent's sexual role brings with it new ambivalence. The mother's first response to the little girl's wanting to be more like her mother may be "What took you so long?" "Why did you ever feel inclined to make fun of me for even a little while?" "Why did you ever question my worth, my talents, my beauty?" Sure, the mother realizes that a special interest in the father need not mean a repudiation of the mother, but it may have felt that way.

Any wariness that the mother feels toward the daughter usually pales in comparison with what she feels about herself. The child identifies with the mother because she needs to be clear about who she is, and she finds out who she is by learning what it means to be a female. Roles are society's ways of providing security. Supposedly, you learn the feminine role so you can act with confidence as a woman. The child is eager to identify with the mother because she seems like such a lovable person, such a successful woman. But while the child may want to become an apprentice, the mother may be far from sure she wants to be a role model, because she may not be sure who she is as a person, and what she is as a female.* The child asks, "Who am I?" and the mother may be wondering the same thing. (Ironically, the mother also wonders "Who am I?"

* Men have similar identification problems, though they haven't been permitted much expression because the male sex is supposed to represent the full human actualization that a woman desiring liberation strives for. The social pressure on the man to assert himself, fight his way in life, be aggressive and not show any feelings takes its toll in higher male suicide and criminal rates, more incidence of illness and early death.[6] The father may be anything but delighted if this is what he has to offer his son. What's more, the father may feel guilty because he doesn't have the opportunity to spend large chunks of time with his son so his child can have sustained contact with a flesh-and-blood man. Instead, the child may learn what it is to be a man by watching TV, reading comic books, seeing cowboy movies, and listening to his mother, who may have many superman fantasies herself.

when her son starts identifying with the father, because her child
may act as if men are the exact opposite of women. The son who
says "Mommy, you must be tired after doing all those *little* things
all day" may prompt the mother to want to change the feminine
image.)

Simone de Beauvoir's words haunt me. She says that "most
women simultaneously demand and detest their feminine condition; they live it through in a state of resentment."[7] I feel this way
myself, but I am scared of the strong words that she uses to describe this sentiment. "Demand," "detest," "resentment"—these
are not feminine, conciliatory, soothing words. A few paragraphs
before the sentence I just quoted, she talks about mothers feeling
disgusted and betrayed when their daughters grow up to be as
weak and ambiguous as they themselves are. "Disgusted," "betrayed"—I am frightened that these feelings will come true, and
my immediate reaction is to want to smooth over any resentment
with a concerted effort to think "contentment." There must be a
good deal of truth in the angry words she uses if I react so strongly
to them. I want to deny these ugly emotions, but my anxiety points
out the truth in what she says.

My trouble is that I have grown up wanting to please everyone;
I want to please myself, society, men, women, and children. I feel
pulled, pushed, and eaten up by the notion that woman's place is
in the home, by the thinking that says a woman should not compete with a man, she should make him aware of what his capabilities are.[8] Yet I find it appealing to pose as the woman who finds
fulfillment in husband and family, who comforts, conciliates,
satisfies, gratifies, encourages, and cheers men and children. But,
on the other hand, I strive to be bold, not just saucy. I want to be
brilliant, not just clever. I want to be creative and original, not just
productive and patient. I have internalized the American belief
that "you can do anything if you try hard enough." But I have also
internalized the fact that women are not supposed to be too competitive, that they should always put their families' needs ahead of
any personal inclinations. I am a walking contradiction. Does my

family come first, or do I? Clearly, it is "better," in some absolute
sense, for a human being to be brilliant as opposed to being just
clever, but women are encouraged not to aspire to brilliance,
because it is "unfeminine." Should a woman strive to be "feminine" or to be a fully developed human? In which direction should
I encourage my daughters to go, so that we will not hate our
mutual weakness and each other, but enjoy instead the strength
and vitality that we see in each other? For me, this is the central
question for the mother to answer when her daughter starts identifying with her.

Strength and vitality are not qualities that the child rearing
literature speaks of. If you read some of the books on developmental issues during the genital period, you will come up against
the same biological-determination propaganda that I talked about
in the first chapter. Consider this advice:

The female tends to be quite concerned about the fact that she does
not have a genital organ like the male, her feelings about it arousing
a state called "penis envy." More than that, the girls are jealous of the
extra prerogatives which being male gives to the boys. There is no question but that having a penis, being a man, gives certain privileges in
our society. *We do not know many women who do not resent this fact*
in one way or another, for which *they can hardly be blamed.* . . . Obviously, for the girl who feels that the boy has more privileges than she
the obvious procedure is to *state the truth to her in no uncertain terms.*
She should be told that she has sexual organs as good as those of the
male, but that *they are of a different kind;* she should be told that she
can have as much pleasure out of life as the boy, despite external differences; that she can grow up and play the role of being a mother, that
she can produce a child, which he cannot, *which is one of the compen-
sations for being a woman.* (Emphases mine.) [9]

Reading this, you get the impression that "penis envy" is an in-
capacitating, chronic condition. Presumably, women cannot hope
to be strong and vital human beings because they are already
physically disabled. Women's inherent weakness, *i.e.,* lack of
certain prerogatives, is accepted as an unalterable fact. The authors

of this book clearly suggest lying to little girls as an answer to the problem; they do not blame women for feeling bad because they are already castrated, but by all means do not tell little girls that. That their lives can be as pleasurable as a man's has about the same note of conviction that a testimonial to the joys of a leper colony might have. What does it mean "to state the truth to her in no uncertain terms"? One wonders what having "as much pleasure out of life as the boy, despite external differences" means. In fact, the references to organs "of a different kind" suggest that women are beings "of a different kind"—maybe even *sub*human, certainly *sub*male. Having a child sounds a bit like getting a Social Security check; it is a compensation for not being self-sufficient. The little girl is not being educated in what she can be but to what she can't be.

There are many, very real resentments that can be reactivated in the mother as the child goes through this stage of development. All those long-forgotten questions about whether your own parents were upset when you turned out to be a girl instead of a boy may start creeping back into your consciousness. If you have a daughter, they are constantly linked with whether you really are contented with having a girl of your own. Have you really come to terms with society's unspoken but very definite dictum that a "good woman" gives her man "boy children?" I remember having a phone conversation with a man after the birth of our second daughter and being told, "Your husband is just like me, not man enough to have boys." That kind of thinking, even if most people are too polite to be so blunt, affects a woman's life from the beginning, and it is bound to surface as a factor in her responses to her children once they start acting like little persons of a specific sex, rather than as neuter babies.

I know that I found myself taking the "rib" story of woman's arrival on this planet very seriously once my daughter started talking about what she would be when she grew up. Are women men's playmates, fashioned from men's bodies and dependent on them because they are the superior sex, or is this another story that men concocted to make themselves feel better because they actually do come from women's bodies? Why don't most authors talk about "breast envy" or "womb envy?" Don't boys feel that they are missing something? Why do the girl's very finished, external genitals get ignored, while boys are encouraged to be proud of their penises? Why does everyone mention the Oedipal period and the boy's relationship with his mother in detail, mentioning the little girl's feelings only in passing: "Girls go through something similar with their fathers and mothers?"

I remember hearing one psychiatrist describe the boy's Oedipal problems as more difficult than a girl's because the girl gets to identify with the beloved mother, whereas the boy has to forsake the beloved mother and identify with the father if he is to grow into a man. I used to feel good when I heard this kind of talk, because I liked the idea of some day being someone's "beloved" mother and because I liked the idea of boys having a rough time growing up to be men. Maybe this kind of language suggests that some psychiatrists are envious of the little girl's possibilities for blessed maternity. But more likely this is another example of how women are told to enjoy the present "good life," whereas men are told that the initiation into manhood will be hard, but the world *will* be theirs.

Little girls are doubly cursed. They are taught what it means to be a woman by women who resent their own femaleness, women who feel the tensions in their social roles, but who usually have not come to terms with whether women belong only in the home or whether they have a place in the world. Even if the mother can offer her daughter the hope of moving gracefully between family life and public pursuits, the girl's future possibilities will still be limited by the prejudices of the community-at-large. What we offer our daughters as models clearly has implications for what they, as mothers, will offer their sons and daughters in the future. The old saying—"It's a man's world; woman's place is in the home"—is an obvious starting point for thinking about sex roles.[10] Do women have a place in the world of politics and economics? Do men have an important place in the home? I believe every parent should think through these questions, because *the educational experience of identification should not be unplanned* if it is important to the development of functioning men and women. What are the advantages and disadvantages of assigning each sex a separate sphere of influence?

If a woman's sphere of influence is to be limited to the home, maybe we should prepare them to be gourmet cooks, lascivious beauties, fastidious housekeepers, human rocking chairs, and give up the pretense of educating them for anything else. We should not encourage them to read anything but cookbooks, sex manuals, vacuum-cleaner warrantees, and child-care rule books, because they might otherwise get the notion that they are not realizing their maximum potential as human beings, and they might want to move away from the confines of the domestic-expressive role. Since women who are cut off from the world might not know what to say to their children and husbands, we should develop scripts for what to say on every possible occasion. All women should take tranquilizers, "pep" pills, and aphrodisiacs regularly so they can manage their passions and direct the emotional traffic in their homes in the appropriate fashion. Any woman who is not pretty enough to attract a man and get a home of her own should have plastic surgery by the age of twenty-five or find work as a governess, housekeeper, or in some factory that makes domestic products (food, clothes, baby bottles, and so forth).

This joyless scenario does not suggest a life much different from the one currently advertised. The "home" represented in the mass media sounds like a good breeding place for schizophrenic, drug-taking children who are as indifferent to the world-at-large as their mothers and who are as condescending to their mothers as their fathers are. It might be infinitely more appealing to get rid of "home," so that both sexes function most of the time in some sort of community (*e.g.,* kibbutz life at its best), rather than leave women stranded in a home sealed off from the outside world. But most Americans might find giving up "home" too communistic for their tastes. (What would our capitalistic society do if several families decided to share a washing machine, barbecue pit, hair dryer, and other appliances?) They would probably prefer some combination of home and world in the feminine role. But how do you combine the two?

Usually little girls are prepared for the world by default. They are encouraged to develop skills they can sell in the market place "just in case" they do not get married. I want my daughters to develop their talents, but not only as insurance against the possibility they never marry. I want them to be pleasing, but not to feel they have to please to win favors. I want them to enjoy the company of men and children, to feel the need for companionship between the sexes and between the generations, but I don't want them to think that they exist only through relationships with others. I want them to enjoy their sexual possibilities but not to feel that they are sexual objects. I do not want them to grow up resenting themselves and their sex. Let them resent instead a society that expects them to live vicariously through their husbands and children without resentment. I want them to be affectionate, understanding, and generous, not because women are supposed to be that way but because these are good human values to encourage. I want them to feel they are a part of the world community, but I do not want them to think that their relationship there can begin only once their household duties are finished.

In the process of figuring out what I want for them, I have discovered what I want for myself. I cannot wave away sexist attitudes and discriminatory practices, but I can give my children a questioning mind and a sense of their own worth. To do this, I need to develop a questioning, open mind and a sense of my own worth. If I want my five-year-old daughter to develop her character rather than become a walking caricature, I find that I have to free myself from stereotyped thinking. I have to rid myself of some of the hackneyed conventions that are part of my mental set. For there are many times when I catch myself thinking just as those psychoanalysts do who define man as a human being and woman as a female; when she behaves like a human being she is said to imitate the male.[11] Automatically, I call the little boy who likes to climb tall trees boyish, while the little girl who likes to have all her cars collide with each other I see as indulging in masculine play. Both are exercising their muscles, their imaginations, and their aggressive feelings, so why do I assign different values to their behavior?

The fact is that I have been indoctrinated from my earliest memory to think that feminine means one set of behavior and masculine another. I am not unlike my friend who responded to her son's hitting my daughter over the head with, "Now stop that; little girls don't like to fight like little boys do." The little boy was feeling angry, hostile, and aggressive; it wasn't an invitation to her to engage in a little roughhousing. Why did his mother assign a positive value to his behavior because he is a boy? Why did she automatically deny my daughter any interest in fighting? Do I want my daughter to marry a little boy who thinks the way this one is being taught to think?

I have to remind myself regularly that just because "the central theme of the preschool-age child's dramatic play is domesticity"[12] that does not mean that little girls are "inherently" domestic. Little girls are taught to think that domesticity is more a part of their personalities than it is of boys, when the truth is that both sexes have such inclinations. In girls, these tendencies are reinforced by compliments—"Just like a big lady"—while boys are encouraged to try new behaviors.

So many authors of books on child rearing point to differences between the sexes as if these behaviors were unalterable and essential to the maturing of boys and girls. Talking about the six-year-old, Stone and Church mention that "boys and girls are learning to like different kinds of activities, and in pursuing these they follow separate paths. Girls continue to play house and begin to like hopscotch and jacks, while boys roam farther, play rougher, wrestle, and learn baseball."[13] When mothers tell four-year-old boys that little girls do not like to fight within earshot of a little girl, it should come as no surprise that boys and girls learn to like different activities. They are *told* to like different activities, and mothers are told to encourage different activities because "masculinity breeds further masculinity, and femininity femininity."[14] But what does that mumbo jumbo do except mold individual inclination into a stereotype?

We are told that beginning at the age of six "boys show an increasing superiority in 'vital capacity'—sustained energy output—and muscular strength."[15] At this time, according to most writers in the field, boys develop a taste for factual literature, while girls prefer fiction. Boys become interested in world events, while girls remain interested primarily in home and community.[16] Boys go through a period when they reject peer relations with girls, whereas girls continue to think of boys as future husbands, even when they are critical of their manners.[17] I used to think that the differences which sprang up when boys tried to be boyish and girls tried to be girlish were inevitable. But I am beginning to think more and more like this:

In woman . . . there is from the beginning a conflict between her autonomous existence and her objective self, her "being-the-other"; she is taught that to please she must try to please, she must make herself an object; she should therefore renounce her autonomy. She is treated like a live doll and is refused liberty. Thus a vicious circle is formed; for the less she exercises her freedom to understand, to grasp and discover the world about her, the less resources will she find within herself, the less will she dare to affirm herself as subject. If she were encouraged in it, she could display the same lively exuberance, the same curiosity, the same initiative, the same hardihood, as a boy.[18]

Why shouldn't girls prefer fiction if their own reality is so circumscribed? If everyone tells them that a husband and children are their ultimate goals, it should come as no surprise that little girls are indifferent to national events. When little boys say that they hate girls, they are simply rejecting an inferior way of life. Their rejection of femaleness, from six until puberty, is infinitely sensible, though I should think not inevitable. It is just a case of "I wouldn't mind marrying a female one day (or having one for a mother), but I sure wouldn't want to be one!"

As my daughters look for role models, I want to be sure to distinguish between "biological identification" and "human value identification." Mothers, as adult women, have a responsibility to teach their daughters about their bodies; it makes sense for me to explain the "facts of life" from my hormonal perspective and to teach my daughters how to fix their hair attractively. But there is no reason why my husband cannot be just as active as I am in our daughter's "human value identification." Both he and I can question children's books that say "Boys invent things, girls use what boys invent. . . . Boys are doctors, girls are nurses. . . . You can't play ball—you're only a girl."[19] I hope they can learn about home and the world from both of us. I see no reason to assume that our girls will be less attractive physically, psychologically, and socially if they grow up thinking that Daddy enjoys wearing flowered ties the way Mommy likes to wear long earrings, if they know that Mommy and Daddy both hate to vacuum the living-room rug, though they take turns doing it, if they perceive that Mommy and Daddy both wanted Red China admitted to a seat on the United Nations Security Council but have somewhat different feelings about the Common Market.

When I ask my husband about his day at work, and he responds by asking me about my own (even if my work has been housework and taking care of the children), my daughter learns that spouses are interested in each other. My daughter may try to imitate my taste for bright colors, but it is my husband's compliments—when I am decked out in red and orange—that convince her that I am worth imitating. There is a *reciprocal* nature to the child's identification with the parents. The daughter wants to be like Mommy because Daddy obviously likes the way she looks and acts, but the mother may encourage the daughter to pun like the father because he has the more developed sense of humor. Parents should maximize the child's opportunities for learning about human values from both parents, if for no other reason than because one parent should not feel completely responsible for the kind of person the child develops into.

One of the biggest problems with designating the mother as the exclusive role model for the girl and the father as the primary one for the son is that the child may grow up to see each of her/his parents as representing two radically different domains, between which no intercourse is possible (except sexual intercourse). Simone de Beauvoir came to view her father as representing the intellectual life and her mother as representing the spiritual life. For her, saintliness could not co-exist with intelligence.[20] In a society like our own, which defines the father as the unemotional money maker and the mother as the nurturing homebody—incapable of neutral judgments—the same kinds of irreconcilable splits often affect the children.

When they reach the age at which skills and hobbies are important to them, I hope that my daughters will be interested in stamp collecting, because it gives you a chance to think internationally, in baking bread, because it gives you a chance to experiment with the chemical properties of yeast, in sports, because the large muscles of the body need to mature as much as the grey matter in the head needs to develop. What is "proper" to boys and girls should be de-emphasized. Instead, we should start thinking about what is essential to *full* human development when children first begin to realize that differences do exist.

Both boys and girls should be encouraged to question existing stereotyped sexual distinctions. It may be that some of the "traditional" (though what falls into this category has changed from century to century) activities that have been considered feminine (*e.g.,* cooking, needlework) or masculine (*e.g.,* taking out the garbage, unplugging a clogged toilet) will still be treated that way, but I do not think that we will have a nation of homosexuals and lesbians if even these behaviors are no longer sex-linked. And isn't that society's ultimate fantasy—that all men will be impotent, all women will turn into castrating unattractive bitches, and no more children will be born if girls are encouraged to build model airplanes and boys are shown how to bake cookies?* I do not think we have to worry about that happening. If both sexes are taught that they have economic and political responsibilities, as well as social and family obligations, there is every chance that we might actually realize the human potential of all concerned—men, women, and children.

Once you start thinking about what is essential to full human development instead of molding children into sexual roles that encourage either growth of the heart or of the mind—but not both in one person—you find that it is just as important to call an end to masculine stereotypes as it is to cry out for women's liberation. Emotional relationships and family affairs cannot be the sole domain of women. Women need to stop defining men's behavior in the home as much as women should be allowed to define themselves in the world. The notion that the "good" man is strong, silent, rich, successful, unemotional, and eager to go to bed with his woman every time he looks at her should go the way of all fairy-tale thinking. We need to work toward a society that allows women success but also permits men to fail, that allows fathers to encourage perfection in their children and mothers not to feel weighed down by their imperfections. All roles have their mirror

---

* For Erich Fromm, "the polarity of the sexes is disappearing, and with it erotic love, which is based on this polarity."[21] Jerome Kagan verbalizes similar concerns:

> The liberation of both women and men from the constraining stereotypes of the past may make it difficult for any heterosexual bond to remain strong for a reasonable period of time. There is a growing mutual understanding among young couples that each is capable of going it alone. The old-fashioned notion that man protected woman in return for the healing power of her love may have placed unjust burdens on both partners, but it allowed them to nurture the belief that they were necessary to each other. When both man and woman believe that their own self-actualization takes precedence over any pressure to salve the wounds of the other, potential commitments become fragile liaisons.[22]

Why do authorities confuse self-*actualization* with self-*gratification* and associate it with a decline in heterosexual desire (or an increase in onanism)? Surely, men and women will continue to be "necessary to each other" if "the healing power" of a man's love is accorded the same dignity as a woman's love.

images; the opposite of the good mother and father are the witch and the ogre. But stereotyped thinking only increases our chances of peopling a world full of bitchy, shrewish women and brutish, machinelike men.

Monroe Freedman, a law professor, eloquently underlined the right our children have to a "healthy personhood" in an article he wrote for the newspaper of the American Civil Liberties Union:

Just as our daughters as well as our sons should have *strength, courage* and *independence,* so should our sons as well as our daughters have *sensitiveness, tenderness* and *gentleness.* Thus in seeking to end the sexist programming of children, the psychological liberation of women is a valid and increasingly recognized goal. But the fundamental civil liberties issue is the equal right of every individual, male as well as female, to become a completely human being—the most basic of all liberation concerns.[23]

Earlier in this article, Professor Freedman also suggested how detrimental male stereotype is to "man's world." For example, some analysts of the Pentagon Papers have noted that male decision makers were reluctant to question any escalation of Vietnam killing, maiming, and devastation because of "masculine pride."

Although I have emphasized in this chapter the mother-daughter relationship through the Oedipal-Electra period, both the mother and the father can use this time to reassess what it means to be attractive and sensuous, to re-evaluate how limited and prejudiced their own thinking may have become. I have mentioned some of the "normal crazy" thoughts, feelings, and fantasies a parent might have during this time. I expect every parent will be able to embroider each of the general themes I have considered with examples and insights of her/his own. Women's liberation-type thinking has occupied an important place in my consideration of sexual role identification, because this seems to me the obvious time in the child's life for stereotyped, discriminatory thinking to be perpetuated in the next generation. To "grow up," the mother has to move beyond any resentment that she may feel about being born female and/or having a daughter to thinking about the role options that she would like to offer her child (male or female) and any changes she might like to make in her own relationship to home and the world. Fathers, too, have role resentments that come to the fore at this time, which should be understood and resolved, if possible. The mother who is sorry she quit school before she developed any job skills and the father who is tired of hearing about what she "gave up" for him have to understand themselves and move beyond resentment to try new behavior that allows for mutual growth and development. After all, you never do "grow up" if you blame everyone else for your troubles. A mother who goes back to school without having to feel "grateful" to the husband who takes over some of the cooking and cleaning chores seems a happier prospect than a resentful one who rears a daughter who hates men "because they take the best years of your life" and a son who despises nagging women.

If we individually start questioning the "feminine mystique" as our children begin to notice sexual differences, will the "motherhood mystique" continue to exist? If ultimate fulfillment for a girl ceases to be defined as maternity, won't we have more relaxed, less depressed mothers, maybe even more thoughtful and capable ones, too? If mothers could become more a part of the world, maybe homes would seem less like isolated fortresses, and maybe the world would be a more "human" place to live in? No one knows the answers, but I think they are good questions.

Helmer. This is monstrous! Can you forsake your holiest duties in this way?

Nora. What do you consider my holiest duties?

Helmer. Do I need to tell you that? Your duties to your husband and your children.

Nora. I have other duties equally sacred.

Helmer. Impossible! What duties do you mean?

Nora. My duties towards myself.

Helmer. Before all else you are a wife and mother.

Nora. That I no longer believe. I believe that before all else I am a human being, just as much as you are—or at least that I should try to become one.

—*Henrik Ibsen*[1]

7

Coming to Terms with Yourself

What does personal awareness mean for a mother? One thing it means is coming to terms with the tensions I have described. This book has alternated between detached analysis and acknowledgment of the poetry of the motherhood experience, between seeing the funny side of a mother's dilemma and the serious issues, between sarcasm and assurances of good things to come. I have attacked the notion that a child can fulfill the parent, but I have also spun out a theory that emphasizes the mutual development of parents and children as one of the benefits of this relationship between the generations. I described the preoccupation that we have with being "ideal" mothers and producing "perfect" children, yet I put forth my own notions of what is "appropriate" and "better." There was mention of the security and comfort derived from learning social roles, but I also emphasized balancing this need for order with the need to move out of stereotypes that choke growth potential. I think mothers should be less self-conscious about each one of their actions causing a reaction in their children, but I also believe consciousness-raising is an essential part of the parent's growth and development. "Angry" and "demanding" are adjectives that describe being a mother as much as "kind" and "generous."

The bittersweet quality of my exposition was no literary accident; it mirrors the tensions inherent in the subject matter. Motherhood (parenthood) is a *"mixed"* bag. There are Spockian tendencies in all of us to see our children as the greatest satisfactions in life, but there is also the inclination to see raising children as too dull an assignment for any "alive" adult to embrace.[2] If anything, I have deliberately wanted to underscore the fact that there are no such things as mutually exclusive thoughts and feelings; it is *never* a case of feeling only one way or the other. When you leave your children for a few days, you hope that they will wave a happy good-bye and not cry over your leaving, but part of you, nevertheless, prays they will miss you *desperately*.

Coming to terms with yourself means gradually realizing what your expectations for yourself and those around you are, what your needs are, and what the unfinished business of your own growing up seems to be. In the process of developing self-awareness about your expectations, you actually learn all sorts of things. A couple of weeks ago, my daughter playfully pushed me and said, "Why can't you be little, like me? We could be such good friends; we would have so much fun playing together." Her comment triggered all sorts of thoughts in my mind: I never realized before exactly how frustrating it must be to have those you love the most so obviously superior to you in size and capabilities. The desire for parity in a relationship is strong indeed. Wasn't my child putting into words what I always hoped about my parents—that some day we would be friends, equals, and fully understand each other? I yearned to be an adult so we could freely exchange ideas, never realizing that as I grew older they, too, were growing older. We were doomed from the beginning to live in a different piece of time.

It hurts to think that the relationship you imagined taking place in some fuzzy future will never be. Having children of your own does not make you *equal* with your parents. You have the fantasy that you can be the mother you always wanted, that your child will be a miniature "you," but that does not work out either. I so much want to be a "friend" to my daughters and share the "fun" my daughter promised, but it is impossible. She will never understand how inept I feel at times, and I will never understand what it is like to be a five-year-old in the decade of the seventies. The best I can hope for is learning to enjoy the sense of promise our moments together have, learning to enjoy the learning.

I have gained some understanding of what Lidz means by developing tolerance.

The individual gains a new understanding and tolerance of his own parents, seeing them now from the perspective of an adult rather than from that of a child. He recognizes that the parents he blamed and resented were also caught in the web of their fates, that they had been spouses as well as parents, that they too had been beset by problems that had interfered with their capacities as parents. The new perspective of the parents . . . modifies the superego and permits greater tolerance of the self and sometimes even of the spouse.[3]

"Caught in the web of their fates" is a phrase brimming with meaning. All three generations—grandparent, parent, and child—are separated from each other and bound to each other by thousands of hopes, frustrations, and resentments. The basic attitude to these relationships must be tolerance, or else the "trapped" feeling will paralyze any forward movement.

There is so much for parents to learn. You learn to stop making up rules: "If my daughters really love me, they will . . . ; if my husband really loves me, he will . . . ; if my parents really love me, they will . . ." As you realize that mothers aren't "experts" in anything—except maybe juggling—you might translate this insight into not expecting your child to be an "expert" ballplayer, which is all to the good, because you don't want your expectations to freeze her/his pitching arm. You learn that negative feelings can be minimized or handled "better," but it does not follow that they can be eliminated. Just because a parent is barraged with advice doesn't mean that one is getting any "answers." The more you explain things to your child (about government, about religion, about discrimination, and so forth), the more you realize what an excellent opportunity you have to rethink issues and become a more discerning individual yourself.

You also begin to be aware that there are very few "natural laws." Roles and rules are made on earth, not created in heaven. (Just think how arbitrary is your own rule that hamburgers are to be eaten at lunchtime, but not at breakfast, and you are bound to have a new appreciation of how contrived and plastic everyday conventions are.) When you read about "inherent principles" or "obvious purposes," you realize that someone, somewhere, is always assigning a value and giving his/her opinions on the matter. But you can learn to join in the fun of describing and prescribing and tell *Parents' Magazine* what makes sense to you and what does not, instead of automatically digesting the written words as if Moses, not some person making a living, were the editor. You may begin to question the theory of "penis envy" in little girls, because they surely have some sense of their bodily integrity long before they notice that penises come in handy on picnics. Or you may come to realize that it is more important for parents of preschool children to think of *role* education than to worry about *sex* education. You may have a new appreciation for the fact that just because this is the way things are, it does not follow that this is the way things *should* be.

And you learn how to ask the important questions: How do you help others develop their potential and use them to enrich your own person? How much understanding do you need yourself to be understanding? How do you support while encouraging independence? How do you balance being efficient with being creative? How do you combine "wanting to be taken care of" with "wanting to take care of?" How do you work with your own angry, destructive impulses without being burdened by the guilt and despair generated by such feelings?

Coming to terms with yourself means realizing all the issues that a mother has to deal with in a given day. You do some chores around the house and talk with your daughter about why it is nice for her to have a sister with whom she can discuss how silly parents sometimes are. Your child asks you why you have a job, and you explain how much you enjoy doing something that interests you and how important it is for girls and boys to decide on a career that satisfies them. One minute, you and your husband are enjoying your child's improvised dance, and the next minute, you are talking about why people are afraid of dying and what it means never to see someone again.

What is the answer to the age-old question "Who comes first, me or my family?" I have decided that it has to be me, and as I become a more mature "me," my family will derive the benefit. Translated, this means that I cannot hope to give if I am not sure whether I have something to give; I have to develop myself just as I develop my children. (It is stupid to ask, "Who comes first?" unless you also ask, "With respect to what?") Life does not end with having a husband and two children. Insurance company charts assure me I have the possibility of forty more years ahead of me. What am I to do with these years? Thinking is often painful, and the more I think, the more it hurts. It hurts me to think that I was foolish enough to believe that being a wife and mother would eliminate my own "growing pains," just as it hurts me to think that I once actually believed the suffragette movement would have gotten somewhere faster if they had only been "more feminine." It hurts me to think that I might want *more* (of *everything*) out of those forty years and not be able to get it. Consciousness-raising is a dead-end street if the possibilities opened up by new awareness cannot be actualized and if the anger generated by understanding existing stereotypes cannot be channeled into constructive behaviors.

Therefore, personal awareness, for all its positive value, is an essentially passive (I am tempted to call it "feminine," but I will resist the impulse) attitude unless it is used to bring influence to bear on society-at-large. You can look into your psyche and try to find meaning in the conflicts you have experienced, hoping that soulsearching will free you to be a better mother. But it is of limited value if you do not also tackle some of society's basic assumptions about women and mothers at the same time. I have tried to demonstrate how the expectations and frustrations of the individual woman are related to the values of the society in which she lives. Let's look at the motherhood mystique once again, this time not just for insights about personal dilemmas, but for the purpose of pointing out the need for a totally different conceptualization of the word "mother."

The first requirement would be for all mothers to realize that the title of Naomi Weisstein's article "Psychology Constructs the Female, or the Fantasy Life of the Male Psychologist"[4] is speaking to them. It is not particularly original at this point in Women's Liberation thinking to mention that women have been described, defined, and circumscribed by men, yet we have not fully realized the ramifications of this for mothers. I would minimize the malice behind these maneuverings. For me, the problem is not so much that mother is seen as a headless pair of breasts or a castrated half-person who has the responsibility for cleaning and toilet training, but that she has come to represent *man's projection of the ideal*. The very word "mother" has all sorts of meanings that bear little resemblance to a real person; it has become a *metaphor*. "Mother" represents a set of behaviors and hopes that no flesh-and-blood woman could ever meet.

If feminine role problems were due only to "woman being defined as nigger" (a comparison that pops up over and over again in the feminist literature), women would have protested their second-class citizenship a long time ago. But women, and most especially mothers, are not chained to present roles by visions of female subservience, but by the notion that they have the inherent where with all to keep everybody "happy," to charm away aggressive feelings with a lullaby, to soothe tired souls, pointing out the joy of day-to-day living. The ties that bind are not so much shackles of male chauvinism as ribbons of fairy-tale thinking. It is hard to say which came first, "the strong, silent man" or the "weak, expressive woman," but both represent the other sex's notion of what the ideal looks like, and the two projections—since they are both so one-sided—have come to be taken as "necessary" conditions for the development of the other.

Erich Fromm, in his bestseller *The Art of Loving*—which shaped the thinking of millions in the late fifties and sixties—personifies the kind of idealizing that I am talking about. His theories are embellished at crucial junctures with symbols and figures of speech that lead to all sorts of absurd conclusions. He says, "Mother's love is bliss, is peace, it need not be acquired, it need not be deserved."[5] "Mother is the home we come from, she is nature, soil, the ocean."[6] "Mother has the function of making [the child] secure in life."[7] Just ponder these flowery words, so apparently full of wisdom, understanding, and promise, and see what every mother is tormented by.

Motherly love . . . is unconditional affirmation of the child's life and his needs. . . . Motherly love . . . makes the child feel: it is good to have been born; it instills in the child the *love for life,* and not only the wish to remain alive. . . . The promised land [land is always a mother symbol] is described as "flowing with milk and honey." Milk is the symbol of the first aspect of love, that of care and affirmation. Honey symbolizes the sweetness of life, the love for it and the happiness in being alive. Most mothers are capable of giving "milk," but only a minority of giving "honey" too. In order to be able to give honey, a mother must not only be a "good mother," but a happy person—and this aim is not achieved by many. The effect on the child can hardly be exaggerated. Mother's love for life is as infectious as her anxiety is. Both attitudes have a deep effect on the child's whole personality; one can distinguish indeed, among the children—and adults—those who got only "milk" and those who got "milk and honey. . . ."
Most women want children, are happy with the new-born child, and

eager in their care for it. This is so in spite of the fact that they do not "get" anything in return from the child, except a smile or the expression of satisfaction in his face. It seems that this attitude of love is partly rooted in an instinctive equipment to be found in animals as well as in the human female.[8]

Fromm's passing mention that he is talking about "ideal types"[9] does nothing to diminish the notion that the ideal can and should be realized. When he says that "the effect on the child can hardly be exaggerated," he dispels any hope that his ideas might be intended simply as provocative ones, and not be taken as gospel. In fact, his use of Biblical symbolism reinforces the impression that he speaks gospel!

Fromm's heavy reliance on metaphors to make his points— home, nature, soil, ocean, land of milk and honey, animals— graphically illustrates my point that the word "mother" has become a supermetaphor, conjuring up all sorts of hallowed images that have little or nothing to do with the functioning of individual female parents. One wonders why his observation that few mothers are happy people does not make him reconsider the direction of his thinking. If happy mothers are a prerequisite for satisfied children, why doesn't he write about how a mother's happiness is achieved? But then his arguments are basically circular; he assumes that happy mothers can only come into being if their mothers were happy (presumably we sit around and await the coming of the Promised One, the "happy" mother). Oh, to be a father! "Fatherly love is conditional love,"[10] therefore, cowlike happiness is not necessary to father's functioning.

Fromm's use of phrases like "unconditional affirmation of the child's life and needs" and "mother's love for life" makes him sound like a little boy browsing for a Mother's Day card. These sentimental, unreal words either describe what he wants his mother to be or what he thinks she wants to hear but show no insight into the stuff of which mother-child relations are made. His call for milk and honey makes me wonder if the LaLeche League should not call a special meeting to consider functionalism and human breasts: If women have *two* spigots, doesn't that mean that they are *destined* to provide milk in one and honey in the other? Why must happiness in the mother-child relationship be equated with animal instinct? Is this because Fromm does not know how else to justify his *inhuman* expectations, except to admit from the beginning that they are not human? Or is it because he is basically the kind of romantic who idealizes nature, and women by extension?

Isn't Fromm's thinking based on the notion that if you say something is (or may be) a certain way long enough and loud enough, then it might even happen? Father will gladly assume a role in child rearing after the age of six[11] because "love for life" will already exist or not exist; he will not be liable to criticism, since it is mother's job to lay the positive foundation. (It has become a psychiatric truism that all later problems are due to mismanagement of the child's first few years.) I do not think that these functional divisions between the mother who gives and the father who guides are simply the result of women getting the short end of the lollipop once again. They represent man's basic desire to escape a complicated and confusing task. They also denote man's hope that someone can do what he knows he cannot do. *

Man desperately hopes that someone is capable of unconditional love, patience, and generosity. There must be comfort, security,

* Mothers are hounded by *idealistic* thinking even when theorists emphasize maternal destructiveness rather than mother love. Though Joseph Rheingold says in his book, *The Mother, Anxiety and Death,* "Mother's love is the prize of death," and "All roads seem to lead to the mother-child relationship as the essential source of the death complex in its catastrophic aspects," he emphasizes mother as "the fundamental agent of individual fate." He maintains that "if men performed the caretaking duties of the mothering person, it is doubtful that they would exert comparable harmful influence because very few men have the destructive drive toward children common to mothers." But he ends his book by declaring, "Only a personality bred of perfect maternal nurturance would fully realize its potentiality." Instead of turning motherhood over to men, or analyzing the absurd pressures that he puts on mothers when he says their impulses ultimately lead to genocide, racial persecution, and human exploitation, he concludes that "Man is inherently capable of cooperation, and there will be less unnatural behavior when the transmission of destructiveness from mother to daughter is meliorated." Dr. Rheingold's important insights into maternal ambivalence (with its destructive components) are completely obscured by his own love affair with mother as omnipotent.[12]

and peace somewhere. Since women seem to be more attuned to nature, why not make them responsible for keeping natural feelings and frustrations at bay, in order that the world of thought, of discipline, of travel and adventure can come to pass? Mother is happiness. Mother is supposed to defuse the aggression that threatens to poison all relationships. It is a beautiful dream, a poetic fantasy, but it is doomed to failure.

It is doomed to fail because women *are* human beings. They are no more patient, generous, loving, understanding, secure, and natural than men are, though both sexes have the potential for learning a wide range of behaviors. No matter how much you want mother to love you without reservations of any kind, it cannot happen, because she is not even a little bit divine. She does not come equipped with a magic wand. The mother's emotional needs, society's expectations of her, and the limits of the feminine role have made her inclined to put all sorts of riders on her affections. Her existence is conditional. Transcendence of self may be a developmental goal, but no one is other-directed without a struggle. A mother is neither a Hegelian plant full of budding passivity nor Freud's mutilated creature in search of a penis substitute nor Pius XII's "crown of creation" and the "expression of all that is best, kindest, most lovable here below."[13] One wonders if there isn't more truth in Germaine Greer's assessment of altruism. "Properly speaking, altruism is an absurdity. Women are self-sacrificing in direct proportion to their incapacity to offer anything but this sacrifice. They sacrifice what they never had: a self. . . . The altruism of women is merely the inauthenticity of the feminine person carried over into behavior."[14]

Fromm's entire philosophy (and he is but one of many who subscribe to these views) is predicated on many falsehoods. Mother represents a life that never was and a world that never will be, *i.e., unconditional* affirmation of the child's life and his needs. No wonder everyone is angry at mother; the ideal is corrupted every minute of the day. Mothers may actually feel inclined to finish a chapter of the book they are reading *before* they answer the baby's cry for food, companionship, or a clean diaper. When the child screams out her/his frustrations, the mother often responds in kind. Mankind's infatuation with mother does not prove that the ideal can be realized, but it surely does prove that the first person with whom the child has extended contact has become the object of a fantastic amount of magical thinking.

What Fromm advocates does not even make sense in terms of what a child needs. The absence of frustration is dangerous, and the complete absence of frustration before the age of six, when he says a child begins to need the father's brand of love, authority, and guidance, is absolutely ludicrous.* That formula seems a sure way to create a generation of narcissistic tyrants. If the father waits to ride in on his stallion the day there are six candles to be blown out, mother and child might well say, "Who invited him to the party?" (Sound familiar?) Fromm underestimates a child's ability to understand that mother has needs of her own: "Mommy wants to be by herself because she is tired of listening to screaming." He underestimates the ability of mother and child to explain themselves to each other: "Mommy feels nasty today, so go outside and play before I start getting mad at you for no reason at all" or "Mommy, I feel tired today; can I bring my blanket down and snuggle with it on the floor?" And he ignores the reciprocal relationship of the mother and father to each other and to the child.

I am more inclined to think the way Abraham Maslow does:

To be strong, a person must acquire frustration-tolerance, the ability to perceive physical reality as essentially indifferent to human wishes, the ability to love others and to enjoy their need-gratification as well as one's own (not to use other people only as means). The child with a good basis of safety, love and respect-need-gratification, is able to profit

---

* In another place Fromm says, "For most children before the age from eight and a half to ten, the problem is almost exclusively that of *being loved*. . . . The child up to this age does not yet love."[15] It is not unusual for authors to *under*estimate the capabilities of children (surely five-year-olds *can* love) at the same time they *over*estimate the importance of the mother. For example, the tradition of the always-available mother is bound to create the expectation that small children always fear strangers. If "mother *is* the euphoric state of satisfaction,"[16] then children are liable to be demanding and pleasure seeking.

from nicely graded frustrations and become stronger thereby. . . . It is via the frustrating unyieldingness of physical reality and of animals and of other people that we learn about *their* nature, and thereby learn to differentiate wishes from facts (which things wishing makes come true, and which things proceed in complete disregard of our wishes), and are thereby enabled to live in the world and adapt to it as necessary. We learn also about our own strengths and limits and extend them by overcoming difficulties, by straining ourselves to the utmost, by meeting challenge and hardship, even by failing.[17]

First of all, one wishes that Fromm and theorists like him had the ability "to differentiate wishes from facts." Then "mother" might refer to a real person and not just to a metaphor. Maslow's mention of *not* using "other people only as a means" is in shocking contrast to Fromm's emphasis on "unconditional affirmation." Is Mother a person or a means to an end? For Fromm, Mother is not a person whose nature we can learn about. She is a smiling, giving face; she is completely outside the world of thought. She *is*. She is not a person in the process of *becoming* more mature. She is an element, just like the soil and ocean that she is linked with. It may seem as if I am being overly hard on Fromm. Isn't his only fault really a misguided use of analogies? If Fromm simply sketched a motherly principle, which is unconditional, and a fatherly principle, which is conditional, in order to show how the mature individual (male or female) is a synthesis of these two antithetic qualities, then you might be right to challenge my criticism. But Fromm not only sees the sexes as "opposite poles"; his idea of the fully mature adult is man. Let me quote at some length from him to illustrate what I mean.

Eventually, the mature person has come to the point where he is his own mother and his own father. He has, as it were, a motherly and a fatherly conscience. Motherly conscience says: "There is no misdeed, no crime which could deprive you of my love, of my wish for your life and happiness." Fatherly conscience says: "You did wrong, you cannot avoid accepting certain consequences of your wrongdoing, and most of all you must change your ways if I am to like you." The mature person has become free from the outside mother and father figures, and has built them up inside. In contrast to Freud's concept of the super-ego, however, he has built them inside not by *incorporating* mother and father, but by building a motherly conscience on his own capacity for love, and a fatherly conscience on his reason and judgment. Furthermore, the mature person loves with both the motherly and the fatherly conscience, in spite of the fact that they seem to contradict each other. If he would only retain his fatherly conscience, he would become harsh and inhuman. If he would only retain his motherly conscience, he would be apt to lose judgment and to hinder himself and others in their development. In this development from mother-centered to father-centered attachment, and their eventual synthesis, lies the basis for mental health and the achievement of maturity.[18]

It is clear that Fromm, like so many other authors, is not using the pronoun, "he," just to be grammatically correct. "He" *does not* apply to "she." The boy may learn giving from the mother and reasoning from the father, but the girl cannot learn reasoning, or else she might not give unconditionally. If the girl synthesizes the two inclinations, she might decide not to be a mother! There is no provision in his system for how a girl might integrate into her person the "fatherly conscience." Judgment, tempered at times by love, is still masculine, but unconditional love, tempered by judgment, *does not exist*. He is implying that girls do not "grow up," because they apparently never cease to be nonjudgmental; they have no *personal* expectations of the child. They are *ipso facto* outside of the sphere of reason, so there is no need to elaborate a growth and development theory that would account for how they came to be "unconditional givers" in the first place. The only hint Fromm gives is that "the woman who is happier in giving than in taking . . . is firmly rooted in her own existence."[19] What "existence?" Doesn't that brilliant insight into rootedness just get you back to mother as metaphor, and the "Fantasy Life of the Male Psychologist?" (Even if you give Fromm every benefit of the doubt and agree with him that he is only talking about "ideal types," you are still left with two questions: Why did he choose *saintly* behavior as woman's goal? Why should he be so specific about the father getting involved in child rearing after the child is six years old if he didn't mean to be taken literally?)

Mind you, if Fromm were the only theorist who condemned the female to being "the euphoric state of satisfaction" in his writings, my analysis would merely be interesting; mothers could continue to function unaffected by his dream world. On the contrary, I have devoted so much space to this exegesis of Fromm's thinking because his words so perfectly illustrate the theoretical and mythical morass surrounding the role of mother, which is reflected daily in popular thinking. Classic Freudian theory also maintains that the girl does not normally integrate the talents of both parents, as the boy does in moving from mother to father, but simply identifies with the mother.* (One wonders how Sigmund Freud explained Anna Freud's success to his friends; maybe he was like most fathers who think their daughters are "different"—the world *should* be theirs.) If the motherly contact is stage one and the fatherly contact is stage two on the way to maturity, then by theoretical fiat a girl is not allowed the same developmental route as a boy. How, then, does she get to be the supermature, altruistic person who is supposed to transcend her own needs regularly for others without reservation? That's the question that never does get answered. Since most theorists treat male behavior as normative (*e.g.,* he has the penis, therefore, having a penis is the norm from which women deviate), how women get to be what they are supposed to be remains a mystery. Women are supposed to be what male theorists think little boys *ideally* need if they are to grow up

---

* Hegel's belief that "women regulate their actions not by the demands of universality but by arbitrary inclinations and opinions"[20] was revitalized by Freud's pronouncements on the Oedipal conflict. For Freud, the super-ego is heir to the Oedipus complex, and, therefore, women do not have developed super-egos by definition: "In girls the motive for the destruction of the Oedipus complex is lacking. Castration has already had its effect. I cannot escape the notion (though I hesitate to give it expression) that for women the level of what is ethically normal is different from what it is in men. Their super-ego is never so inexorable, so impersonal, so independent of its emotional origins as we require it to be in men."[21] Freud made the phallic synonymous with the human and excluded women from *full* personhood.

and be strong, adventuresome, and reasonable. Mothers are super-duper projections of their fantasies and desires.

Sadly enough, no one ever asks what women *need* to be all-loving and all-generous. Women are not seen as fellow human beings but as *preconditions to men*. Concepts about women are treated as assumptions or givens in the central theory that is male-oriented. *Woman is a means to man's ends.* Woman is elevated to the status of a natural ideal (her behavior is instinctual), only to be ignored because she supposedly does not have to go through the developmental struggle that men have to go through to *achieve* the ideal. And she is also told by the theorists that women are less ready to submit to the great exigencies of life,[22] so she can't aspire to becoming the truly successful person a man can. She could not do it if she tried, and what's more there is really nowhere for her to go.

This excursion into the idealized fantasies that we have about mothers has not been an academic exercise without practical significance. Mothers' lives are touched by metaphorical thinking all the time. They are told they can warm their children like the sun, be fertile like Mother Earth, and are counseled that pregnant women experience a "nesting" instinct like the birds do. But when mothers are described as "holy vessels," they may start wondering if they aren't just big pots. When reminded that "nature intended them to have children," they may simply feel like robots without wills of their own. Pick up any greeting card meant for mothers and think about the romanticized, extravagant sentiments expressed in a few lines of merry jingle; you will gain a new appreciation for how unreal the role has become. The illusion that "the hand that rocks the cradle rules [by soothing] the world" may be very gratifying at times, but it is more likely to be terrifying when you realize how little your own behavior measures up to the projected ideal.

It goes back to what I said at the beginning of this book: if you assume that mothers are *already* grown up, adequate, or mature, then you are not thinking about how to grow up, how to become more adequate and more mature. Motherhood is a role you must grow into over time, bit by bit. There is nothing automatic about it. No one can be happier giving than getting all the time, in spite of psychiatric decree.

Woman is locked into the role of giver because male theorists want to define her as *gratified* by what the other sex *disregards*.[23] One of the biggest fears that the current Women's Liberation Movement has uncovered in men is that women might demand the self-interest which has previously been only a male prerogative: "As men and women gradually develop the same profile of needs, total self-interest becomes a dangerous reality."[24] Instead of worrying about female self-interest, it makes sense for both sexes to have the same goal for the adult years: moving from healthy self-love to shared intimacy with a loved partner, and on to helping the next generation do the same.

You cannot affirm a child's life if there is no corresponding affirmation of your own life and needs. But there is nothing instinctive about coming to terms with yourself—your strengths and failings, your expectations and your needs. Nor is there anything instinctive in using this learning to help your child grow and develop into a whole personality. It is hard work that only becomes more and more impossible to effect if you keep waiting around for milk and honey to flow from your person. In fact, women might be inclined to be more generous and loving if this response wasn't written off all the time as something mothers *automatically* do.

Coming to terms with yourself, then, means that society's fantasies have to be plucked out of your unconscious and be brought to the conscious level, where you can see them for what they are. To the extent that "mother" is a metaphor for perfect love and nurturance, *it is not even someone you can hope to be*. Poof! No more mothers. Maybe we should bury the word and the fantasies and start talking about female parents instead? For coming to terms with yourself as a mother also means working toward new options in "parenting" and going *beyond* the motherhood mystique.

When we and our culture and our religions agreed to hold woman the inferior sex, cursed, unclean and sinful—we made her mom. And when we agreed upon the American Ideal Woman, the Dream Girl of National Adolescence, the Queen of Bedpan Week, the Pin-up, the Glamour Puss—we insulted women and disenfranchised millions from love. We thus made mom. The hen-harpy is but the Cinderella chick come home to roost: the taloned, cackling residue of burnt-out puberty in a land that has no use for mature men or women. Mom is a human calamity. She is also, like every calamity, a cause for sorrow, a reproach, a warning siren and a terrible appeal for amends. While she exists, she will exploit the little "sacredness" we have given motherhood as a cheap-holy compensation for our degradation of woman: she will remain irresponsible and unreasoning—for what we have believed of her is reckless and untrue. She will act the tyrant—because she is a slave. God pity her—and us all!

—Philip Wylie[1]

8
Beyond the Motherhood Mystique

Only when individuals constantly question whether their present expectations allow for growth and development and follow questioning with *demands* for social change to encourage the maximization of human potential will we get anywhere. (A mother can feel angry that society expects the impossible of her, but her occasional wrath will not change the *status quo* any more than being able to recognize a put-down at thirty paces will.) I have already suggested that a world beyond the motherhood mystique might conceivably not include any mothers; it would be peopled instead by *female* parents and *male* parents. I would like to elaborate on why I think "parenting" should replace mothering (or fathering) as a description of the generative function and why a developmental framework demands that each individual adult in society look upon working toward new options in life styles as an essential part of her/his maturity.

I have already spelled out many of the reasons why one should do away with the word "mother." The word no longer refers to a woman but describes some imaginary element of nature in female form, who unconditionally affirms the child's life and needs. Mom is expected to be everything her children and the child-rearing "experts" want her to be. She has come to mean a person "destined" to live vicariously; her only hope for "fulfillment" is in finding a penis substitute, a baby. Mother in our society has also become so equated with failure that it is questionable whether any self-respecting person would want to assume an identity riddled by so much guilt and responsibility.* It is no wonder that Shulamith Firestone looks forward to childbearing being taken over by technology.[3] But it isn't because of all these depressing, negative associations that I would recommend the change in nomenclature. If I thought any new word would automatically clear the air of existing stereotypes, then I could just as well sit down with a ouija board and come up with a new one.

For me, being a parent—it can refer to either mother, father, or another interested adult—presupposes a totally different philosophical base; it assumes that humans of both sexes have an interest in establishing and guiding the next generation. I see the role of parent as a function of the adult years akin to Erikson's talk of generativity. (For him, generativity leads to a gradual expansion of ego interests in order to avoid individual stagnation.)[4]

---

* Rheingold underscores this when he says, "It will not do to speak of 'parents.' The use of the terms *parents*, the *caretakers*, and *the human environment* in discussing infantile experience strikes me as an evasion of assigning sole or preponderant responsibility to the mother."[2] Everyone seems eager to reduce the troubles of "the human environment" to the mother's sins of omission or commission.

"Parenting" doesn't conjure up romantic images of complete self-sacrifice; it does imply sensitivity to the needs of the next generation, kindliness, protectiveness, continuity of care, and respect for the dignity of children. The word suggests some sort of equal and/or reciprocal relationship between the mother and the father in their dealings with their children. Once you think of parenting, rather than mothering or fathering, you are free to question some of the basic assumptions about the nuclear family, to consider some of the economic underpinnings beneath present life styles, and, most important, you are free to think about how to divide the task of parenting in new ways that might develop the growth potential of all concerned.

The two-generation family—the nuclear family—is a recent invention. From primitive tribes through most of the history of Western civilization, the extended family was the norm; couples married and moved in with their parents, cousins, sisters, and brothers. If you didn't live in the same house, you lived next door or just up the road, or at least in the same town. Until the Industrial Revolution most people lived in small towns, villages, or on family farms (theirs or some rich man's) where everyone knew everyone else. Except for the privileged class, everyone (including children) was expected to help out in the fields and with household chores. Children tended to see a good deal of their grandparents and other over-forty relatives. Grandmother might be baking bread while keeping an eye on a sleeping child, and grandfather might be spinning a yarn for the village youngsters, while *both* parents were harvesting crops. If your children wandered over to watch the blacksmith shoe a horse, you didn't have to worry about strangers, because most neighbors would watch out for your children. In those days there were no television sets to lull children into passivity, no toy and food commercials to make you feel inadequate as a provider. At its best, agrarian life was amicable, harmonious, and comfortable; at its worst, it was stifling, factious, and poor.

But pastoral virtues and vices were torn apart by industrialization. The sexes were frequently segregated during working hours; home and job became separate geographical units; men spent the day relating to machines instead of to other men; people clustered in cities full of asphalt and strangers; and families were herded from one part of the country to another in search of more money. There were benefits, too. Large numbers of relatives did not have to share limited goods; couples could hope for their own apartments and furniture. More people had more things than ever before. Young men had occupational alternatives to following in their fathers' footsteps. Travel, shopping junkets, university education, urban culture, and other advantages that had previously been open only to the wealthy, seemed so much more desirable than living all your years in the same rural county.

Couples craved a home of their own because they could now afford one, but also because they yearned to free themselves from the influence of their parents (in twentieth-century America this also came to mean wanting to be free of the parents' "Old Country" customs and ethnic values). The nuclear family came into being for economic reasons, but the promise of parents getting along with their children—if they did not have to contend all the time with the physical presence of their own parents and siblings—made the nuclear family more popular than it might have otherwise been. There was the sincere hope that the "good life" could and would materialize if family rivalries and grievances could be ignored except for holiday visits. Surely two adults who love each other can live happily ever after if they don't have to live with anyone else but their own children! The growing dehumanization of industrial work (*e.g.,* one man may spend eight hours each day just installing steering wheels on an automobile production line) and the increased turmoil of urban life (*e.g.,* firemen now worry about rocks being thrown at them when they're putting out fires) made happy families seem especially necessary. The home came to be seen as the last warm haven in a hostile world of steel and glass, and family closeness was idealized.

Ecological awareness, contraceptive information, and the high cost of beef had some impact on further limiting the nuclear family to only *two* adults and *two* children.* Four seemed like a good balanced number for promoting mental health: each adult would have a partner, each child would have a partner, and, it was hoped, each sex would have an opposite number. Since there were to be only two adults in each household, it seemed especially important that the workload be divided between them. There was more and more talk of complementary roles—separate but equal—between the husband and wife so that angry, aggressive feelings would be minimized. As one psychiatrist put it, "The division into four role allocations according to generation and sex reduces role conflict within the family."[5] Harmony between the sexes was promised if men and women just wouldn't compete with each other.[6] The experts conceded early on that you do not have freedom from role conflict if you happen to have children of the same sex,[7] but they failed to realize until more recent times that life is not easier if you keep avoiding feelings by cataloguing them or by making arbitrary divisions of labor seem like divine edicts. Instead of blessing us with order and solace, the nuclear family has isolated individuals into tiny ghettos of confusion and loneliness. The nuclear family seems to have exaggerated many of the feelings it was supposed to help us forget.

Life is not easier when women are given total responsibility for home life in exchange for economic support. Competition and rivalry do not go away if you are sealed off from the outside world. If you ban overt aggression, it turns into passive aggression when you are not looking. Aggression needs to be directed into activities, but if your only activities are child-centered ones—as Mother's traditionally are—then you are in big trouble. Philip Slater put his finger on some of the deep-seated problems of the mother's role in the nuclear family when he said:

* The ideal of the big, happy, healthy family persists even though we are aware of the tensions in an extended family. One of the reasons the Kennedy clan has so dazzled the American public is that the members of such a large family actually do seem to get along with each other. It is easy to assume that if they can comfort and support each other, they can do the same for the nation.

In our society the housewife may move about freely, but since she has nowhere to go and is not a part of anything anyway her prison needs no walls. This is in striking contrast to her pre-marital life, if she is a college graduate. In college she is typically embedded in an active group life with constant emotional and intellectual stimulation. College life is in this sense an urban life. Marriage typically eliminates much of this way of life for her, and children deliver the *coup de grâce*. Her only significant relationship tends to be with her husband, who, however, is absent most of the day. Most of her social and emotional needs must be satisfied by her children, who are hardly adequate to the task. Furthermore, since she is supposed to be molding them into superior beings she cannot lean too heavily upon them for her own needs, although she is sorely tempted to do so. This is, in fact, the most vulnerable point in the whole system. Even if the American housewife were not a rather deprived person, it would be the essence of vanity for anyone to assume that an unformed child could tolerate such massive inputs of one person's personality. In most societies the impact of neuroses and defects in the mother's character is diluted by the presence of many other nurturing agents. In middle-class America the mother tends to be not only the exclusive daytime adult contact of the child, but also a contact with a mission to create a near-perfect being. This means that every maternal quirk, every maternal hang-up, and every maternal deprivation will be experienced by the child as heavily amplified noise from which there is no respite.[8]

Slater very succinctly points out how the individual mother's functioning is tied to the organization of society itself. The stifling isolation of the mother, stranded on her domestic island, is reinforced and extended by the impossible burden that the mother bears in being almost completely responsible for the happiness of her children and for the relationships of the family members with each other. No wonder so many adults feel forever scarred by mother's death-grip caress; children are all that some mothers have, now that motherhood has become a full-time occupation for adult women.

It is a shame that Slater's insights are seriously weakened by his phrase "if she is a college graduate." Though he explains his own middle-class emphasis in the preface of his book, I think that it would be unfortunate for any reader to get the impression that only the college graduate experiences emotional and intellectual stimulation in her prechildren years. The prevailing assumption is that women who don't go to college are still happy with "feminine," passive, hearth-centered goals and have no problems with them, or at least are too dumb to know it. His qualification reinforces the notion that motherhood imprisons only women who are articulate enough to say that they feel jailed, when the truth is that the traditional setup puts *all* women in an impossible role.

Slater's mention of "the presence of many other nurturing agents" in "most societies" underscores the need for thinking about parenting rather than mothering, because as Bruno Bettelheim says, "It is not a proof of love to spend every minute of the day with another person."⁹ In fact, Slater's observation that a mother's constant and exclusive involvement with the child leads to neurotic behavior and not to a self-assured and secure child is a powerful contrast to Fromm's analysis. Unrelieved intimacy can be a depersonalizing experience, because there is the tendency to dilute the closeness by turning off the "heavily amplified noise." For example, the mother who routinely asks her child, "Do you love me?" may eventually be relegated to the status of a broken record. If the *same* person tells you day in and day out to put away your toys after you have finished playing, you may "tune out" the message and the person. The mother's "orders" may seem more like personal idiosyncrasies than habits that deserve cultivating. The mother winds up caught between wanting to diffuse this absurd intensity while persisting in the belief that her undivided attention is necessary to the child. She doesn't want to appear omnipresent and to direct all of her child's conversations, but she peers out the window to see if she should intervene in every squabble over who gets to ride the bicycle next. The mother looms over the child's life, while she feels herself more and more a shadow.

It is a circular trap. *The more a mother is the only adult contact a child has, the more important that contact becomes. The more a child is the only contact (or purpose) a mother has, the more intense and intrusive her behavior will be.* Every action and reaction are magnified out of proportion to reality. Since every gesture and every comment seem so vulnerable to criticism, both the child and the mother try to hide behind neutral habits, stylized conventions, passive responses, and a blank face. Their attempts to neutralize their behavior are rarely successful, I would think, because resentments build up in a relationship with no escape hatches, and strong words spill out even when you are consciously trying your best to contain them.

Instead of producing congenial kinship, the nuclear family has removed mothers, fathers, and children from the active group life that flourished in the extended family. It has exaggerated the relationship between mother and child and transformed differences between the sexes into irreconcilable separateness. It is not only women who suffer from this development. Insights into the social isolation of all of the family members suggest new perspectives on the child's Oedipal-Electra period. *For the more a child has a single male and a single female as the sole view of the adult world, the more the child will be inclined to read sexual conflict into every discord.* Arguments between mother and father (which are more likely to occur if neither knows what the other is doing) are interpreted by the child as proof that men and women can't agree; they don't think and feel the same way. Fights between a single brother and a single sister are viewed as basic incompatibility between the sexes. The struggle at the heart of the Oedipal-Electra period is more likely to be an issue when the family structure assumes as normal an absent husband and the wife at home hungering for social contact. The child's interest in the parent of the opposite sex puts a strain on the fragile balance of the nuclear family, because it brings out some of the aggression and conflict that roles were supposed to control. For example, the mother who spends all day in the company of children may bitterly resent having to "share" her husband with her daughter in the evening, when she finally has the opportunity to have an adult conversation. A son's attention and solicitude may be encouraged by the mother if she feels that he is the only person who understands her needs. The supposed solution to these strains—eventual identification with the parent of the same sex—assumes an importance that it might not otherwise have if the tensions did not exist against a backdrop in which every thought and feeling is distorted by unrelieved intimacy.

Role allocation according to sex is not a very effective means of reducing conflict within the family. There is something very suspect about reducing conflict by emphasizing the differences between two individuals rather than exploring the aggressive and loving feelings they have in common. Toward the end of his book Slater mentions that "it has taken us a long time to realize that seeking to surpass others might be pathological, and trying to enjoy and cooperate with others healthy, rather than the other way around."[10] This insight seems to me to have a good deal of meaning for the nuclear family. The more we divorce the two adults of the nuclear family from contact with each other, and children from contact with *both* parents, the less likely we will be to cooperate and enjoy each other. I remember listening to several women talk about how they had to keep their husbands working because they would not know what to do with them around the house. It is not an uncommon sentiment, but how sad. Their words suggest men can be lovers, but not friends. Isn't this partly the result of a society that values boys growing up to be "masculine" and girls growing up to be "feminine" more than it does both sexes growing up to be *fully* human?

If the nuclear family is not working out, why don't we do something to change things? That is the next question to consider. Even discounting the mumbo jumbo that maintains "a man can be a man only if a woman is a woman" or "a father can be a father only if a mother is a mother," we still have to consider the economic underpinnings beneath present life styles. The nuclear family does not exist just because behavioral scientists hoped at some point it would be a good incubator for healthy children. The nuclear family is essential to a product-oriented society. Simply put, if there weren't so many individual households, there would not be a big market for so many stoves, carpets, dishes, toys, televisions, and knickknacks. If wives did not stay home and baby-sit, cook, clean, and wash the clothes, husbands could not go out and conquer the world. Mother is an economic institution; "in official capitalist terms, the bill for her economic services might run as high as one-fifth of the Gross National Product."[11] (Others have calculated housewives' services to amount to *one-fourth* of the current level of GNP, or $250 billion.[12])

Half the population has to keep things warm and cozy so the other half can go out and think, and master the industrial dragon. Engels put it well when he said:

The modern individual family is founded on the open or concealed domestic slavery of the wife, and modern society is a mass composed of these individual families as its molecules. In the great majority of cases today, at least in the possessing classes, the husband is obliged to earn a living and support his family, and that in itself gives him a position of supremacy, without any need for special legal titles and privileges. Within the family he is the bourgeois and the wife represents the proletariat.[13]

I am not denigrating man's work when I point out that it is founded on the domestic slavery of the wife. My main emphasis is to demonstrate how his work is accorded dignity while woman's work is taken for granted and ignored. If you act like a maid, you get treated like a maid.

Mother's work leaves her with little tangible evidence of achievement. The most elegant meal gets eaten, scrubbed floors invite mud, children always need one more kiss. Garbage piles up, groceries must be perpetually replenished, and someone is always getting a cold or just getting over one. It is easy to feel apologetic and unproductive. But these feelings turn to rage when you pick up the *Dictionary of Occupational Titles,* which defines some 22,000 occupations on a "skill" scale from a high of 1 to a low of

887. How do mothers stack up against hotel clerks, who have a rating of 368? Homemakers, foster mothers, child-care attendants, and nursery school teachers all share a listing of 878.[14] Apparently, the United States Labor Department thinks that mothers are about as low as you can get! (It clearly doesn't think much of children either.)

Not only is mothering considered to be an "unskilled" profession, but women are supposed to work without financial remuneration. Woman's reward is supposed to be security and love, but this reward exacts a price of its own, gratitude. It seems a woman should be *honored* that the man *lets* her manage the budget and *gives* her a *generous* allowance. If a woman wants a savings account of her own, the man usually regards her request as an insult to his ability to give her what she wants, not realizing that her independence has been sacrificed more than his pride. The whole economic relationship between man and woman rarely gets questioned, because it is regularly covered over by a cloud of romanticism: "If our love is true, then we don't have to worry about such incidentals." "Dearest, if you really love me, you will not be afraid to lean on me." "Darling, if you truly love me, you'll be happy that I am successful and you won't need a career of your own." "Isn't being a wife and mother career enough for any woman?" Women are taught to value love and relationships above all else—much more than money, independence, adventure, or fame—so few would argue with this brand of logic.

The notion that woman will provide certain *very difficult* services (which are not even highly valued) in return for the *patronage* of the man is an economic fact of life that needs examination and rethinking. Men hope to find fame and esteem in the world; they are required to act with restraint and dignity. What price does this exact from women?

From time immemorial it has been a part of woman's role to offer men the place in which to act out their feelings, to authenticate them, and in the end to determine and pronounce on their significance.[15]

Bed and board seem poor payment for the responsibility of validating emotions. If women are to function as psychiatrists, maybe they should get similar pay? It is no wonder that the woman who unconditionally "affirms" her children, who "authenticates" her husband's experiences, is constantly worried about failing at her job. No wonder mothers complain of feeling "empty."

This emotional trafficking is as much of an economic issue as money for services rendered is. Both sexes need to give and get the *same* kind of rewards. Concrete values should be placed on woman's work, and the marketing of emotions that characterizes the nuclear family should be eliminated. No one should have to prostitute herself/himself by supplying feelings in exchange for money. Sympathy, solace, authentication, and encouragement are attitudes both sexes should develop in their relationships with each other. Emotions—the buying and selling of love—cannot become the currency of the nuclear family if we really want our children to grow up to appreciate human values. When relationships become possessions—in the words of one commercial, "My wife, I think *I'll keep* her"—affection becomes a commodity, and emotional manipulation and blackmail flourish. It should come as no surprise that the mother who is treated as a possession by husband and children will become the possessive, demanding woman that Kenneth Keniston describes in *Youth and Dissent*.[16]

Putting a concrete value on mothering or housekeeping is problematic when you try to get down to specifics. Though proposals that would assure the wife a salary for housework (being legally entitled to a specified percentage of the husband's salary) have considerable appeal, most of these plans still make the husband the wife's *employer*.[17] Schemes to pay the mother for taking care of her children still have as their rationale the romantic ideal I have criticized: "It is a rare and exceptionally gifted woman who does something more important in the outside world than she does during those critical first six years when she is helping to form the personality and character of a child."[18] They reinforce some impossible notion of the available, all-generous woman. Personally,

I am committed to certain principles that don't lead to any *one* solution: (1) Some things are done out of love, and it is a mistake to attach a monetary value to these behaviors; (2) Women should have their own economic connections to the community-at-large so they aren't always dependent on their husbands for money; (3) Housekeeping and child-rearing responsibilities should be shared by both spouses, since the former is too boring for any one person to have to do, and the latter is too much responsibility for only one person to have.

Relationships between the generations are also too often predicated on emotional rewards, with gratitude as payment. The mother exacts a price for her devotion: "You owe it to me, after everything I've done for you, all I've given up for you." This might not be so costly if the child didn't take her away from all other rewards (*e.g.*, a paying job, community work, social contacts, political involvement). Do not be misled by my use of so many business words to assume that I am only playing with economic metaphors when I talk about the buying and selling of emotions. I sincerely believe that woman's obligation to make husband and child feel good in exchange for her physical and emotional security is as much an economic issue as whether all adult women can be absorbed into the work force. Acknowledging the monetary value of keeping a house clean or providing tax credits for child care will not put an end to domestic slavery if the one-sided, give-get nature of emotional exchanges is not also altered. Women deserve status and money, but they also *deserve* affection, personal affirmation, and understanding.

So where do we go from here? Probably the first thing I should do is point out that the nuclear family is not as bad as I might have made it seem in the last few pages. It provides the opportunity for long-term relationships that may help to work out the unfinished business of growing up, enabling one to evolve into a giving, loving individual. It forces one to learn how to behave maturely and to try to transcend one's own existence. In the process of underlining what I think its main problems are (the insane intensity between mother and child, the mistaken notion that role allocation by sex reduces family conflict, and the domestic-emotional slavery of the wife), it is too easy to make the whole situation sound like Sartre's play, *No Exit,* where hell is defined as a place where one is trapped with people who torment you by their every word and silence. Some families are like that, but there are also many families ahead of the textbooks, whose members are already experimenting with ways to minimize some of the problems I have considered.

More men today willingly provide nurturing to their children—be it singing a lullaby or kissing a bumped head—than any of the current literature would seem to suggest. However, it is important to put the problems into words and to recognize them for what they are, even if they do not fit your personal situation, because these basic problems may affect how you *feel* even when they do not affect what you *do.* The mother who does not spend all day at home with her children because she cannot stand the isolation may continue to think she is a bad mother because society still expects the preschool child's mother to stay home. And her husband, who gladly encourages her to do what she wants to do, may still wonder if some women cannot handle being a mother *better* than his wife can. It helps to know the truth of the matter is that it is an impossible job for all women as presently defined.

What would a brave new world without these problems look like? I have already suggested that it would be one peopled with *female* parents and *male* parents, because no one sex, and no one person, should be responsible for nurturing and encouraging the development of the next generation. It would be a world where individuals could recognize fantasies and wishful thinking for what they are and not believe they might have had a problem-free existence if only they had had the right mother. *The magic of conception and birth would be disassociated from magical thinking about motherhood.*

Authorities would no longer talk about a mother working only if "she had an ideal arrangement for her children's care,"[19] because everyone would know that there is no such thing as an "ideal arrangement." Baby-sitters and contacts outside the nuclear family would be encouraged *for the sake of the child,* not just as a clandestine convenience for the parents. Everyone would realize that it is just as important for the child to feel that there are more than two adults in her/his world as it is for the mother and father to have regular contacts outside the home. Parents would be able to talk to their children about baby-sitting arrangements without communicating their own guilt and uneasiness to the child. Men would all come around to thinking the way Dr. Spock now says he does:

Women should have as much choice as men as to where their place will be. . . . If a mother wants an uninterrupted career, it is up to the two parents to decide, without prejudice, how to divide the child care or get part-time assistance from a grandmother or a suitable sitter. I admit my sexism in having previously assumed that the mother would be the one who would limit her outside work at least to part-time until her children are 3.[20]

In fact, in my brave new world, "part-time assistance" could come from the grand*father* (if only they survived male competition more often) without anyone thinking him a peculiar or unusual man.

Schools would not assume that mothers are sitting around the house always available to pick up children when a half-day session is declared without any advance notice; half of all nursery school teachers and baby-sitters would be male. Women would not have to become pregnant to stop working at a job they did not like, and a man could let his wife be the primary breadwinner without her being called a "ball breaker" or him being called "effeminate." Women would not "have to" work to get out of the house either. Arrangements would be available in each community so that a parent could get good care for the child if he or she just wanted to get away for a few hours of privacy. (In Columbia, Maryland, each neighborhood has morning and afternoon nursery school programs, and ninety cents-per-hour day care is available on a part-time basis.) [21]

Society would realize that there are different kinds of work and that no one sex should be assigned one or two areas to the exclusion of others. In fact, every individual might consider having some limited economic connection with society-at-large, while putting aside some time for parenting, recreation, community action, and maintenance work. It is not a question of women becoming more like men but of the work ethic changing for *both* sexes. Each parent might spend twenty or twenty-five hours a week earning money (we're moving toward shorter work weeks already), one day a week in household-maintenance activities (cleaning, laundry, shopping, cooking), ten hours a week working on community projects (cooperative day care, schools, care of the aged, and so forth) and the rest of the week in traditional leisure-time activities. (Single adults would also have community obligations.) Exactly how a couple would divide their time would be negotiated between the partners, but some connection with the economic sphere, the local community, activities between the generations, and household upkeep would be expected of each person. Their preschool children would have to spend only part of each day in a day-care facility, because they could spend the rest of the day at home with one of their parents.

The notion that there aren't enough jobs to go around if all adult women work would be dismissed as irrelevant if society reorganized economic functioning to take into account the other developmental needs of women and men. Efficiency would cease to be regarded as the ultimate criterion of a good society. Instead, "the pursuit of happiness" might be valued much more than it is at the present time. The "leisure-time problem" would be a non-problem if society accorded parenting and regular community involvement the same dignity that it does economic pursuits. The discriminatory aspects of part-time work (no pension benefits, seniority not acknowledged, no opportunity for advancement, and so on) would end if most workers were not chained to the forty-hour week. Janeway even suggests that work for women might serve as an escape valve to marriage-as-an-institution in much the same way that adultery, prostitution, and divorce have in the past, because work can provide constructive stimulation and a rise in one's self-esteem. Whether or not you take seriously her humorous remark "that a paycheck will be as satisfying as an orgasm,"[22] it is important to realize that some sense of fulfillment rarely comes from being interested in only one thing.

Day-care facilities could be drastically improved if they were no longer considered the preserve of the poor or the deviant members of society. For example, if you stop worrying about whether to encourage day care and put your energy instead into thinking of new day-care structures, you might try combining family-style care (three or four children in the care of one adult) with larger activity groups. An emphasis on neighborhood support of the family might move the whole approach to day care away from 8 A.M.- to-6 P.M. institutional rigidity to a friendly grass-roots effort. If all the parents of preschool children devoted their community time to work in a cooperative care facility (covering, say, a ten-block area), children would have ample opportunity to see their own mothers and fathers and the parents of their friends. The children's environment would be truly stimulating (or at least as stimulating as parents can make it), each parent would have an opportunity for time without children, and next-door neighbors might even get to know each other.

Parents should continue to have ultimate responsibility for their children, but society has an *obligation* to integrate parents *and* children into everyday life—whether this means allowing maternity and *paternity* leaves at work, permitting parents to work half-days so they can be half-time parents, or encouraging businesses to provide day-care facilities so parents can have lunch and coffee-breaks with their children. For years, French law has required every community with a population of more than two thousand to provide an *école maternelle* for children up to six years of age; almost every community has its *crèche* for infants as young as two months.[23] These social supports *have not* ripped apart the fabric of family life, as President Nixon feared widespread American day care would, but these programs have enabled those French women who want to, to have a family and career without fear of ostracism. If the first six years of life are as critical as the experts say they are, then *our highest national priority* should be thinking of new ways to maximize children's development during those years instead of dumping this responsibility exclusively on mothers. And cross-cultural studies suggest that adjustment is most facilitated when the child is cared for by *many* friendly people.[24]

In my brave new world, Parents' Day cards would read, "I love you so much that when I'm mad at you, I know it is only a passing feeling." Parents would realize that good relations between the generations means that a thirty-year-old woman can say to her four-year-old daughter, "I wonder why I have been feeling so fussy today?" and have the child reply, "How should I know why big people are fussy sometimes? I haven't figured out why little people are sometimes fussy!" On the other hand, a mother who said to her five-year-old son, "Go out and play house; you can be the daddy and be the boss," would be considered a throwback to sexist times. The little boy next door would not say to my daughter, "Here comes your Mommy," as my husband walked by, just because he was taking care of our children for an afternoon.

Popular books would cease to be dedicated to the wife for providing "the *usual* wifely tolerance and support for my efforts." Commercials that show the man fumbling with dishes and children while the wife is away would be illegal, because they simply reinforce the notion that women find easy what men either don't want or can't do well. Newspapers would no longer carry stories describing welfare mothers as "*just* sitting home with their children," because everyone would know that parenting is hard work. Pictures of the "ideal" nuclear family would not always depict the *first*born as a son, the *second*born as a daughter. Authors would be penalized for their patterned thinking if they wrote as one did, linking Simone de Beauvoir's decision to write her most famous work, *The Second Sex*, with Sartre's suggestions to her while puffing on his philosophic pipe: "It even took a man to provoke this moment of Damascene revelation."[25] In fact, social scientists might give considerable thought to whether present envy between the sexes is immutable or whether these conflicts "merely mark a transitional moment in human history."[26]

Other professionals might notice, as Maslow has, that one of the characteristics of loving mature couples is that they do not make sharp differentiations between the roles and personalities of the two sexes,[27] and growth and development books would not end with ambiguous messages like this one:

And, of course, we still cannot say what is cause and what is effect, the extent to which such preferences arise spontaneously out of being a boy or a girl or the extent to which the child accepts them as appropriate to his or her sex. It is likely that children might often enjoy activities assigned to the opposite sex but are restrained by a sense that to do so— or even visibly to want to do so—would be a betrayal of their sex role. . . . We must further consider that boys in our society are oriented toward active mastery and control of the environment, whereas girls take on a more passive accepting orientation. . . . Although we should like to be able to go even further toward understanding and explaining sex difference, it is not necessarily with the aim of reducing them: almost everyone will agree that such differences have decided virtues. An understanding of sex differences will contribute, however, to our more general knowledge of how people develop and of how we can further development. Meanwhile, it appears that the ancient jingle still has some truth: Snips and snails and puppy-dog tails, that's what little boys are made of. Sugar and spice and everything nice, that's what little girls are made of.[28]

Snips and snails, sugar and spice, indeed. How can you "further development" or find out what the human potential of both sexes is if you continue to see with the blinders of stereotype? What it means for a man to be warm and loving might look different from what it means for a woman to be warm and loving, but we will never find out how to describe these real differences if we have well-known professionals telling us that boys and girls are not made of the same molecules and human needs.

In the future that I wish for, "Wait until you have children of your own" would stop being the threat one generation hits the other one over the head with. Couples would make up a new family name when they got married, so they could develop a *mutual* identity instead of the woman borrowing the man's. The grammatical "he" would be abolished, so every author would be forced to figure out whether the subject under discussion is "she," "he," or "she/he." And each generation would know that it had a unique role to play out in its own time: "What the older generation then urgently wished for itself, but had to acknowledge as the hope of the future—this is the legacy of youth. That the preceding generation wished to create such a better world makes it a worthy standard for youth."[29]

Everyone would realize that there need to be periods of experimentation to find out what life-style options are really best for a particular family. Some mothers might continue to function as primary parents—at least in terms of the number of total hours spent with the children—but different parenting options would be encouraged by the society-at-large on the assumption that developing one's human potential can often be accomplished by different people in different ways. For example, two families might buy a three-story house, and each could have one floor to themselves and one floor for common activities. The advantages of the nuclear family could be retained, but the children would have regular, planned contact with four nurturing, teaching adults. Architects might experiment with building apartment houses having "common rooms" on each floor. Families might decide that a modified "extended family" experience is the best way of handling the parenting pressures of the preschool years. Even if the average commune only lasts for one year, it might be exciting to live with some single men and women and another family for a year, sharing the maintenance and parenting work. (It also makes considerable economic sense, since these are the years when young parents can least afford to get outside help.)

Everyone will have to approach these issues from a slightly different place in history. Individuals vary considerably in how much they might be willing to experiment with new life styles, depending upon how they themselves were brought up. But part of growing and developing is realizing that other points of view, other options do exist or should exist. Frankly, I am not willing at this point in time either to give up my house and move into a commune or to invite others to move into my family. But I deliberately make a point of giving my children varied contacts with a number of people, old and young. I have had twelve-year-olds come in and play with my children while I do some work on the second floor, so my daughters will have the experience of playing with older children. When my husband and I are both working, our girls have regularly gone to another family's home, so they can have the opportunity of playing with other children and seeing how other parents relate to each other and their children.

I do not think I have to provide my children with diverse experiences that might be uncomfortable for me, but I certainly feel an obligation to encourage the flexibility of mind that permits new possibilities. If my children are to mature and if my husband and I are to mature, we have to develop some sense that we are all part of society and that, as such, we cannot permit life styles and roles to remain restrictive; otherwise our own promise will be stifled. De Beauvoir says that "humanity is something more than a mere species: it is a historical development; it is to be defined by the manner in which it deals with its natural, fixed characteristics, its *facticité.*"[30] I feel that way about parenting. It is a creative process which becomes an unbearable burden if relationships are fixed by a set of rules that show little or no understanding of real feelings, pressures, and needs. If parents cannot openly demonstrate to their children the potential they have for dealing with their own lives, how can they help their children deal with their possibilities? If Mother is someone who has to put off a *full* life "until the children are grown up," how can that woman encourage growth?

Freud believed that a woman of thirty seems incapable of further development, while a man of the same age is at the beginning of his best period of achievement.[31] Though he ignored the cultural pressures (which his own theories in fact reinforced) contributing to woman's inertia, his observation certainly supports the impression that the period of childbearing has traditionally been more of an end for women than an important beginning. In Victorian times, a rough equality between the sexes existed until puberty, then post-World War I women were encouraged to lead free, interesting lives until they were married. Now the goals of the larger society are open to women until they become mothers. *Moving beyond the paralyzing, romantic idealism of the motherhood mystique is the final frontier for women.*

If women are allowed to extend their interests and men are permitted to develop their sensitivities throughout their child-rearing years, there is every chance that we might have a better society—a decrease in adolescent rebellion, fewer immature marriages, more effective fathers, less maternal interference and domination of children.[32] Motherhood might actually become the beginning of a woman's best period of achievement, for all adults need to know what parenting teaches:

The uniformity of an infant's needs in its earliest days affects the attendant mother with some uniformity. One learns (or learns to use) patience, intuitive insight and imagination, to enjoy the immediate moment in anticipation of change when it comes and the miracle of potentiality that it points at. One learns a good deal about time—that it passes and yet remains solid as experience. One learns that life changes even if one sits still, when it's wise to sit still, and when it isn't. Most of all, one learns other people and one's own limits in terms of relationships with them. All this is important learning, but let us once again refrain from supposing that it is learned only by women and valuable only to them. *It is the kind of knowledge that is learned on the way to maturity no matter how the path winds.*[33] (Emphasis mine.)

Ironically, as we learn about the *limits* of the role of mother, we won't be so constrained by the weight of global responsibility. We will be better able to seize the liberating moments in the parenting experience that help us grow and save ourselves from being suffocated by the musty rhetoric of the past.

I hope I have made it clear just how much there is for each parent to learn on the way to maturity. Whether my brave new world will ever come to be, I do not know, but part of being a parent is to imagine a brave new world for the next generation and to come to terms with the limitations and possibilities of your own world. There were historical reasons for traditional female/male roles, but there are even better reasons for changing our social institutions and cultural values so that genuine human relatedness can be realized.[34] As I search for words to tie up the thoughts of this book, I find I keep humming one of Mr. Rogers' songs, which goes something like this: "As your fingers grow, and your hands grow, and your feet grow, the rest of you grows, because you're all one piece." I think I will end by paraphrasing his jingle this way: "As the mother grows and the father grows, the children grow, and the society grows, because we're all one piece."

Notes

1. THE MOTHERHOOD MYSTIQUE

1. Simone de Beauvoir, *The Second Sex* (New York: Bantam Books, 1952), pp. 493–94.

2. Germaine Greer, *The Female Eunuch* (New York: McGraw-Hill Book Co., 1970), pp. 232–33.

3. Una Stannard, "Adam's Rib, or the Woman Within," *Trans-Action* 8:1–2 (November–December, 1970): pp. 24–35. Ms. Stannard's article is full of references to the notion that woman equals womb, especially p. 32.

4. Mike Royko, *Boss* (New York: E. P. Dutton & Co., 1971), p. 196.

5. Wilder Penfield, Preface to J. C. White and W. H. Sweet's *Pain and the Neurosurgeon* (Springfield, Ill.: Charles C. Thomas, 1969), p. viii.

6. A. Alvarez, *The Savage God* (New York: Random House, 1972), p. 23.

7. *Ibid.*, p. 26, p. 22, p. 27, p. 30.

8. *Ibid.*, p. 39.

9. Theodore Lidz, "The Effects of Children on Marriage," in *The Marriage Relationship: Psychoanalytic Perspectives*, ed. S. Rosenbaum and I. Alger (New York: Basic Books, 1968), p. 123.

10. *Webster's New World Dictionary,* college edition (Cleveland: The World Publishing Co., 1962), p. 585.

11. Clara M. Thompson, *On Women,* ed. Maurice R. Green (New York: New American Library, 1971), p. 112.

12. Stannard, *op. cit.,* p. 32.

13. Thompson, *op. cit.,* p. 33.

14. Alvarez, *op. cit.,* p. 13.

15. Elizabeth Janeway, *Man's World, Woman's Place* (New York: William Morrow and Co., 1971), p. 57.

16. Louise Bates Ames, *Child Care and Development* (Philadelphia: J. B. Lippincott Co., 1970), p. 273.

17. Morris Zelditch, Jr., "Role Differentiation in the Nuclear Family: A Comparative Study," in *Family, Socialization and Interaction Process,* ed. Talcott Parsons and Robert F. Bales (Glencoe, Ill.: The Free Press, 1955), pp. 314–15.

18. Haim G. Ginott, *Between Parent and Child* (New York: The Macmillan Co., 1965), pp. 170–71.

19. *Ibid.,* p. 169.

20. Zelditch, *op. cit.,* p. 314.

21. Kenneth Keniston, *Youth and Dissent* (New York: Harcourt Brace Jovanovich, Inc., 1971). In this book, the author says that alienated students have expressive, emotional mothers and "weak, inactive, detached and uninterested" fathers. The implication is that the mothers caused the fathers to act ineffectively (pp. 181–85). There is a whole psychiatric tradition that defines the child's problems by the mother's excesses rather than the father's absences ("the schizophrenegenic mother"), when such parental behavior might just as easily be turned around to emphasize a mother struggling to fill a void and father shirking any responsibility for his children.

22. Joyce Brothers, *Woman* (New York: Macfadden-Bartell, 1961), pp. 113–14, 117.

23. Janeway, *op. cit.,* p. 196.

24. *Ibid.,* p. 87.

25. Jerome Kagan, *Understanding Children* (New York: Harcourt Brace Jovanovich, Inc., 1971), p. 26.

26. Janeway, *op. cit.,* p. 162.

27. Evelyn Millis Duvall, *Family Development,* 3rd ed. (Philadelphia: J. B. Lippincott Co., 1967), pp. 193–95.

28. Boyd C. Rollins and Harold Feldman, "Marital Satisfaction Over the Family Life Cycle," *Journal of Marriage and the Family*, 32 (1) (February, 1970), p. 25. This article also points out that the father is most dissatisfied during the time when he is about to retire. It should come as no surprise that men and women experience a high level of negative feelings when they are going through a period where they are "non-people." The difference is that women "retire" very early in life.

29. *Feelings of Conflict in New Parents* (Columbus, Ohio: Ross Laboratories, 1969), p. 6.

2. WHY HAVE BABIES?

1. Benjamin Spock, *Baby and Child Care* (New York: Pocket Books, Inc., 1957), p. 5.

2. De Beauvoir, *op. cit.*, p. 484.

3. Erik H. Erikson, *Childhood and Society* (New York: W. W. Norton and Co., 1950), p. 228.

4. *Ibid.*, p. 366.

5. De Beauvoir, *op. cit.*, p. 484.

6. *Ibid.*, p. 485.

3. THE ANGER-DEPRESSION-GUILT-GO-ROUND

1. Doris Lessing, "To Room Nineteen," in *A Man and Two Women* (London: MacGibbon and Kee, 1963), pp. 277, 278, 279.

2. Brothers, *op. cit.*, pp. 123–24.

3. Ames, *op. cit.*, p. 201.

4. M. Esther Harding, *The Way of All Women* (New York: G. P. Putnam's Sons, 1970), p. 158.

5. Betty Friedan, *The Feminine Mystique* (New York: Dell Publishing Co., 1963). See pp. 11–27, especially p. 25.

6. Lidz, *op. cit.*, p. 128.

7. Norman L. Paul, "Parental Empathy," in *Parenthood: Its Psychology and Psychopathology*, ed. E. James Anthony and Therese Benedek (Boston: Little, Brown and Co., 1970), p. 347.

8. Therese Benedek, "The Family as a Psychologic Field," in *Parenthood: Its Psychology and Psychopathology*, p. 131.

9. Erikson, *op. cit.*, p. 234. The notion that the adult has unfinished business from previous developmental periods is part of Erikson's eight

stages of man, *e.g.*, trust versus mistrust, the baby's first social need, can be reactivated when the young adult is working through the issue of whether she/he can trust the sexual partner in an intimate relationship.

4. THE BETTER PART OF ME

1. Benedek, *op. cit.*, p. 131.
2. *Feelings of Conflict in New Parents*, p. 5.
3. Ann Richardson Roiphe, *Up the Sandbox* (New York: Simon and Schuster, 1970) p. 12.
4. Benedek, *op. cit.*, p. 130.
5. *Ibid.*, p. 130.
6. Irving D. Harris, *Normal Children and Mothers* (Glencoe, Ill.: The Free Press, 1959), p. 139.
7. De Beauvoir, *op. cit.*, p. 480.
8. *Ibid.*, p. 483.
9. Ames, *op. cit.*, p. 207.
10. Georg Hegel, *Hegel's Philosophy of Right*, trans. T. M. Knox (Oxford: Oxford University Press, 1942), p. 117.
11. *Ibid.*, p. 115.
12. *Ibid.*, p. 263.
13. *Ibid.*
14. Roiphe, *op. cit.*, p. 54.

5. BEING IN CONTROL

1. Philip Slater, *The Pursuit of Loneliness* (Boston: Beacon Press, 1970), p. 64.
2. Samuel Z. Klausner, *Two Centuries of Child-Rearing Manuals*, the technical report submitted to the Joint Commission of Mental Health of Children, Inc. (University of Pennsylvania: Project "Hydra," October, 1968), p. 121.
3. Harding, *op. cit.*, p. 158.
4. *Feelings of Conflict in New Parents*, p. 6.
5. Janeway, *op. cit.* See pp. 88–9 for a further discussion of why women have such a penchant for soap operas and advice columns.
6. De Beauvoir, *op. cit.*, p. 487.

7. Slater, *op. cit.*, p. 67. Slater is full of allusions to American society as a product-oriented one.

8. R. D. Laing, *The Politics of Experience* (New York: Ballantine Books, 1967), p. 113.

9. *Feelings of Conflict in New Parents,* pp. 10–11.

6. AND HOW DID JOCASTA FEEL?

1. R. D. Laing, *Knots* (New York: Pantheon Books, 1970), p. 14.

2. O. Spurgeon English and Gerald Pearson, *Emotional Problems of Living* (New York: W. W. Norton and Co., Inc., 1955), p. 79.

3. Roiphe, *op. cit.*, p. 17.

4. *Ibid.*, pp. 13–14.

5. De Beauvoir, *op. cit.*, p. 491.

6. Olof Palme's views on these identity problems of men can be read in "The Male Sex Role: Keeping the Man in the Home," *Civil Liberties,* No. 287 (May, 1972), p. 4.

7. De Beauvoir, *op. cit.*, p. 489.

8. Janeway, *op. cit.*, p. 48.

9. English and Pearson, *op. cit.*, p. 88.

10. Elizabeth Janeway's entire book, *Man's World, Woman's Place,* is devoted to an overall analysis of the social mythology that has developed different spheres of influence for the two sexes.

11. De Beauvoir, *op. cit.*, p. 47.

12. L. Joseph Stone and Joseph Church, *Childhood and Adolescence: A Psychology of the Growing Person* (New York: Random House, 1957), p. 151.

13. *Ibid.*, p. 218.

14. *Ibid.*, p. 225.

15. *Ibid.*, p. 226.

16. *Ibid.*, p. 229.

17. *Ibid.*, p. 218.

18. De Beauvoir, *op. cit.*, pp. 261–62.

19. Myra MacPherson, "Challenging the Books that Teach Girls 'Their Place,'" *Washington Post* (June 6, 1971), p. G1.

20. Curtis Cate, "Europe's First Feminist Has Changed the Second Sex," *The New York Times Magazine* (July 11, 1971), p. 32.

21. Erich Fromm, *The Art of Loving* (New York: Harper & Row, Publishers, 1956), p. 15.

22. Kagan, *op. cit.*, p. 25.

23. Monroe H. Freedman, "Equality: Men's Lib," *Civil Liberties*, No. 287 (May, 1972), p. 4.

7. COMING TO TERMS WITH YOURSELF

1. Henrik Ibsen, "A Doll's House," in *The Collected Works of Henrik Ibsen*, Vol. VII, trans. William Archer (New York: Charles Scribner's Sons, 1906), p. 147.

2. Ellen Peck, "The Baby Trap," *Cosmopolitan*, 170 (6) (June, 1971), p. 82.

3. Lidz, *op. cit.*, p. 126.

4. Naomi Weisstein, "Psychology Constructs the Female, or the Fantasy Life of the Male Psychologist," in *Up Against the Wall, Mother*, ed. Elsie Adams and M. L. Briscoe (Beverly Hills: Glencoe Press, 1971), pp. 176–92.

5. Fromm, *op. cit.*, p. 39.

6. *Ibid.*, p. 42.

7. *Ibid.*, p. 43.

8. *Ibid.*, pp. 49–50.

9. *Ibid.*, p. 41.

10. *Ibid.*, p. 43.

11. *Ibid.*

12. Joseph C. Rheingold, *The Mother, Anxiety and Death* (Boston: Little Brown and Co., 1967). See pp. 15, 103, 107, 151, 204, 209.

13. W. B. Faherty, "Catholic Teaching on Women," in *Up Against the Wall, Mother*, p. 12.

14. Greer, *op. cit.*, p. 148.

15. Fromm, *op. cit.*, p. 40.

16. *Ibid.*, p. 38.

17. Abraham H. Maslow, *Toward a Psychology of Being*, 2nd ed. (New York: Van Nostrand Reinhold Co., 1968), p. 200.

18. Fromm, *op. cit.*, p. 44.

19. *Ibid.*, p. 52.

20. Hegel, *op. cit.*, p. 264.

21. Sigmund Freud, "Some Psychological Consequences of the An-

atomical Distinction Between the Sexes (1925)," *Collected Papers*, Vol. 5, ed. James Strachey (New York: Basic Books, 1959), p. 196.

22. *Ibid.*, p. 197.

23. Kagan, *op. cit.*, p. 26.

24. *Ibid.*, p. 26.

8. BEYOND THE MOTHERHOOD MYSTIQUE

1. Philip Wylie, "Common Women," in *Up Against the Wall, Mother*, p. 80.

2. Rheingold, *op. cit.*, p. 89.

3. Shulamith Firestone, *The Dialectic of Sex* (New York: Bantam Books, 1970), p. 238.

4. Erikson, *op. cit.*, p. 231.

5. Lidz, *op. cit.*, p. 128.

6. Ginott, *op. cit.*, pp. 176–77.

7. Lidz, *op. cit.*, p. 128.

8. Slater, *op. cit.*, pp. 68–9.

9. Bruno Bettelheim, *Ladies' Home Journal* (September, 1971), p. 36.

10. Slater, *op. cit.*, p. 133.

11. Firestone, *op. cit.*, pp. 207–8.

12. Ann Crittenden Scott, "The Value of Housework," *Ms.*, 1 (1) (July, 1972), p. 57.

13. Frederich Engels, "The Monogamous Family," in *Up Against the Wall, Mother*, p. 206.

14. Crittenden, *op. cit.*, p. 57.

15. Janeway, *op. cit.*, p. 196.

16. Keniston, *op. cit.*, pp. 181–85.

17. Crittenden, *op. cit.*, pp. 56–9.

18. William V. Shannon, "A Radical, Direct, Simple, Utopian Alternative to Day-Care Centers," *The New York Times Magazine* (April 30, 1972), p. 85.

19. Spock, *op. cit.*, p. 570.

20. Benjamin Spock, "Woman's Place," *Newsweek* (August 23, 1971), p. 4.

21. Linda Franke, "How To Make Trouble," *Ms.*, 1 (1) (July, 1972), p. 28.

22. Janeway, *op. cit.*, p. 224.

23. Zelda S. Klapper, "The Impact of the Women's Liberation Movement on Child Development Books," *American Journal of Orthopsychiatry,* 41 (5) (October, 1971), p. 730.

24. Margaret Mead, "Some Theoretical Considerations on the Problem of Mother-Child Separation," *American Journal of Orthopsychiatry* 24 (3) (July, 1954), pp. 471–83.

25. Cate, *op. cit.*, p. 40.

26. De Beauvoir, *op. cit.*, p. 674.

27. Abraham H. Maslow, *Motivation and Personality* (New York: Van Nostrand Reinhold Co., 1954), pp. 245–46.

28. Stone and Church, *op. cit.*, pp. 227, 230–31.

29. Bruno Bettelheim, "The Problem of Generations," in *The Challenge of Youth,* ed. E. H. Erikson (New York: Anchor Books, 1965), p. 106.

30. De Beauvoir, *op. cit.*, p. 674.

31. Thompson, *op. cit.*, p. 135.

32. Alice S. Rossi, "Equality Between the Sexes: An Immodest Proposal," in *The Woman In America,* ed. Robert Jay Lifton (Boston: Houghton Mifflin Co., 1964), pp. 98–143. Ms. Rossi paints a very appealing portrait of the "new woman" on pp. 138–40; her well-researched article mentions a number of social benefits for men, women, and children that might result if sexual equality ever becomes a reality.

33. Janeway, *op. cit.*, p. 150.

34. Rochelle Paul Wortis, "The Acceptance of the Concept of the Maternal Role by Behavioral Scientists: Its Effect on Women," *American Journal of Orthopsychiatry,* 41 (5) (October, 1971), pp. 733–46. See Ms. Wortis's article for a fine discussion about the creation of alternative life styles; she makes the important point that changes in the maternal role might lead to changing the kind of children we raise.